ON **Life's** Little Twists AND Turns

ON **Life's** Little Twists AND Turns

Bill **HAYWOOD**

PARTRIDGE
A Penguin Random House Company

To order additional copies of this book, contact
Toll Free 800 101 2657 (Singapore)
Toll Free 1 800 81 7340 (Malaysia)
orders.singapore@partridgepublishing.com

www.partridgepublishing.com/singapore

Contents

Contents

Acknowledgements

This small offering is dedicated to five people and one academic institution who made the fairly dramatic changes in my life possible.

The academic institution involved was Ruskin College in Oxford who made a second attempt at a formal education possible. The College, and more importantly the people within it, were fundamental to what followed over the almost thirty years of my working life after becoming a student there.

To my sister Edna whose financial assistance, and more importantly her encouragement, helped start me on the path to further and higher education during the latter stages of my life and, what turned out for me to be a world-changing way of life.

To my Cambridge Extension College supervisor, Sam Rouse, whose early prompting during correspondence courses offered the encouragement to stretch myself mentally and, to look beyond the then current way of life which was crucial to my eventual academic achievements.

To Professor Christopher Freeman, ex-Director of the Science Policy Research Unit, Sussex University, for growing in me the hunger for research, a true gentleman and scholar.

To Archie Hill, poet, writer and journalist, for providing the realisation that what is current is not necessarily the future, and that change is possible with the appropriate direction and desire.

Finally, to Professor Audrey Mullender ex-Principal of Ruskin College Oxford, for her encouragement in publishing this document and for her generosity in proof-reading the draft of the book*.

* Following the proof-reading some small additions were made to the text, therefore any errors in interpretation, spelling, grammar or syntax are entirely of my own making.

Preface

I am not famous, nor am I rich or influential, so why should I have the effrontery to try setting down the details of my life? Not through vanity or the belief that I can obtain financial reward, given that I am now 75 years old and beyond any dream of riches, but in the hope that, somewhere within these meanderings, a small element of hope might emerge within the thoughts of one or two of the readers, if readers there ever be?

My beginnings were not bright, and my background was not likely to bring forth ideas of anything other than work in factories for the rest of my life. My education as a child was limited, and I left school at the age of 15 with no paper qualifications to my name. Neither I nor my teachers expected anything else of my future than a life of working in factories. However, one's background and early education are not necessarily the precursors of one's life. Events can change, opportunities may arise which cannot be predicted, and luck may play a major part in how that life develops.

The premise has been put forward, and endlessly discussed, that when a child is born it does so 'tabula rasa'. That is, with a clean slate or clean sheet for a mind. As life progresses, it is suggested that this slate becomes imprinted with the child's experiences. This leads to the debate about which is more important in a child's development: 'nature', i.e. the innate character of the child, or 'nurture', i.e. the education, training and rearing or upbringing of the child. Some children are born into relatively affluent families, this may perhaps give them significant advantages as they grow, based on the wealth of their parents; others are born into less fortunate families with fewer opportunities. However, the abilities of all of these children are disparate and not necessarily governed by their ultimate good fortune, in the sense of wealth or otherwise in their parentage. Not all of the children of wealthier families are blessed with the innate abilities that the good fortune of birth brings them. Not all of the less fortunate are condemned to the mediocrity of life due to their upbringing and lack of opportunities earlier in their development.

The educational system in the United Kingdom does not provide, perhaps never has provided, equal opportunities for this latter group of children; the system that exists does not provide the development opportunities afforded to that group. Vast numbers of children are thus cut off from providing the skills and progress that the country requires, simply through being so disadvantaged by their lack of wealth, and because of the perversities of the governors of the country at any one time. Why is the challenge of education unmet in the UK? Governments have a unique role to play to ensure that all members of a generation, poor as well as affluent, have a chance. Everyone deserves such a chance and society needs to help people to secure it. Governments pay lip service to this but the realities of their time in control of the country limit their chances of doing so, or so they claim. Strange how funds can be found to carry out the policies that benefit that party and its followers, while they have the power to do so.

When I read that such and such a group of people, in say the financial services area, have to be paid huge salaries or they will leave the country and go elsewhere, I despair. Why are we hostage to such blackmail? Simply because there is a vast untapped group of people who could take their place given this lost opportunity! If already large salaries are insufficient to keep people in post, why not replace them from the larger pool of trained personnel? It is not difficult to look around the rest of the world and see countries where the impact of higher and further education equal opportunities has been so influential, such as, Sweden and Germany. These are countries that have invested heavily in their educational and health programmes over many decades and, it is no surprise that they are leaders in many fields. Large percentages of their populations have higher and further educational qualifications, compared with the UK.

A hundred or so years ago, Sweden was thought of as the 'poor man of Europe'. During an era when, on one side, there was the development of communism and on the other of fascism, Sweden took a third route by focusing its limited resources on educating and providing health services for its citizens. While, currently, people complain about high taxation there, where would they be without an initial focus in these fields? Likewise Germany, for well over one hundred years has educated and trained its people to high standards, leading to it now being the strongest economy in Europe, and a major player and leader in the European Union.

When you read this, please do not suggest there are no intelligent and able adults to take the place of the more avaricious in our society. The United Kingdom is blessed with people of ability who, in many cases, lack the wherewithal to use it, due to the fact that deficiencies in the educational system have left them unable to develop their skills and talents. Given the appropriate education we have the resources, but it seems we do not have the inclination to use them. This has become even more apparent given the current recession; in fact, the support for education has become less available over recent years rather than greater, despite the efforts to deny this. Successive governments have failed to grasp the opportunities to use the potential of these disadvantaged groups of individuals. It would seem that, in the current environment, the already wealthy are afforded even greater advantages while, for the people lower down the social scale, this gets worse instead of better.

What follows below is my own small story. I write this not in any sense to boast at my own good fortune or to claim that it results from having abilities greater than others (actually I would disclaim this), but hopefully to illustrate to others that there are people out there who could perform, given the opportunities currently denied them, and to ask when the structure of wealth distribution and educational equality will allow this to happen? I make no apologies for focusing a great deal of what follows not just on the story of my life, but on the social conditions that have fostered my fairly strong opinions, particularly those on education, religion, politics, sport and social division. Should these strong views and emphasis offend you, perhaps this book is not for you.

My own little story

Ten years or so ago, at the age of 65, I retired. I made myself a promise then never ever again to 'do another tap' for the rest of my life. For those unfamiliar with the expression in this context, it simply means never to work again. Not for financial gain, nor for charitable reasons. Perhaps such a goal is selfish as far as making a contribution to charitable causes is concerned, but fifty years of more or less full employment meant I felt that I had earned the right to sit and gaze at the ocean, to have a cold beer close at hand, and to enjoy reading a good book. Such an attitude, I suppose, could be called selfish but this old brain is not as clear and concise as it once was and, frankly, I can no longer be bothered to push myself to the fore. Writing this little piece of work helps pass the time and it just may be of interest to one or two others, and may raise some interest in looking at their world in a slightly different way, with a resultant hope of change for themselves.

I love to read and have done so from an early age. I suppose its curiosity and was, and still is, a desire to learn, though in my younger years it comprised mostly cowboy or science fiction novels. Later, it became more educational and is now simply for the sheer pleasure of reading a good book. I guess, I have always had an enquiring mind and perhaps need the stimulation of reading. I can get very bored unless something grabs my attention. These days, of course, we are told that the written word in its paper form is outdated. Youngsters just log on to the computer to read—if they still do read. Rather, it seems to me that for many they prefer to sit in front of a computer playing games or watching a television set. I have younger relatives who seem to prove the point to my satisfaction. For me, there are few more pleasurable things than the tangible feel of a newspaper or book in my hands. Newspapers are read cover to cover. Could it be that, even at my advanced age, I have an enquiring mind and still want to learn new things?

Perhaps five years service in the Royal Air Force in the 1950s and 1960s, where two rules were considered important amongst us lower ranks, led to my current reluctance to volunteer for anything. The first rule was not too important to my 'tap' decision, it was 'Don't stand still for too long or someone will come along and paint you blue': in other words, just keep moving and do not focus too much on work, and that is my first excuse. The second RAF rule was important, however, it was, 'Never volunteer for anything'. Regardless, I recently spent a sleepless night thinking about events in my life and, at the age of 75 and looking at the state of many young people's live's as expressed so widely in the media, I thought that there were a few little things that a willing recipient might wish to take on board, and that maybe could be considered a charitable act on my part!

However, the major reason for putting these few words down, was 'Never be too certain that you know exactly where life is leading you', you never know, and I certainly could never have guessed as far as I was concerned. The first half of my life was what I would have imagined it to be on leaving school, that is a life of factory drudgery. The second half turned out to be diametrically different. Another thing that has been very much to the fore in my mind in recent years is that 'You're never too old to learn something new'. In my case that was also certainly true, following my time taking correspondence courses, followed by being a mature student at Ruskin College and then at Sussex University. This proved the maxim to be true, at least as far as I was concerned.

Perhaps, in writing this autobiography, I speak now mainly to those people I would place into the second or less fortunate group of people I mentioned above:

those who were born without wealth and into what is termed the working class, and from which group I count myself fortunate to have sprung.

I note that, in 2013, the current UK Prime Minister, David Cameron, urged working class people to raise their sights and ambitions. Given that it now costs a fortune to attend university, in part barring the less wealthy from entrance, that the funding of schools has become very basic and that many teachers seem now to be somewhat vilified by some government ministers, this is a bit like cutting off someone's feet and then telling them to stand up. A nice analogy I believe!

Childhood

I was born in 1938, and our house was one of many in terraced Sydenham Road, Smethwick in the West Midlands. There were three bedrooms, though the third could better be described as a box room with room only for a single bed and, virtually no other furniture. There was a front room for Sunday best, which contained a piano that no one could play and an Aspidistra plant in the bow window. Not sure why, but the ownership of a piano and an Aspidistra seemed to be an indicator that you were at least equal to the next door neighbours, if you had such items! Even in our little community people strove to be, if not better then the people next door, at least equal to them. Strangely enough, this little front room was very infrequently used, even on Sundays; perhaps only when a relative popped over for an irregular visit. The living room included a huge coal-burning fireplace that seemed to take up at least half of one wall. It was the usual system for those times in such a home: a cast iron monstrosity, complete with side ovens and trivets hanging over the open fire for the big black kettle to hang upon.

You often see such fireplaces in black and white films showing old style cottages and, in some of the kitchens of the more wealthy country folk—though in the latter case more likely to be an Aga. That fireplace had one major advantage apart from its ability to produce boiled water and bake cakes: it burnt almost all of the time, even at night when banked up with what amounted to small fragments of coal and damp coal dust. The whole house was kept warm. Eventually, that fireplace was ripped out and thrown away, to be replaced by a small open fire surrounded by ceramic tiles and with a couple of tiny shelves, very popular in the 1950s, but a miserable little thing that gave little comfort. I believe the old iron one would now fetch a considerable sum of money for anyone wishing to add character to their homes, though it would require a fairly substantial property to house it without it overshadowing the rest of the room.

There was also a leafed table, heavy and cumbersome, that my parents had probably had from the time they married. Incidentally, for both of them this was their second marriage, and this marriage produced five children of whom I was the youngest. I also remember there were two, five- or six-foot-long glass walking sticks on the wall. These were made of two strands of glass, one white one blue, which were twisted in a spiral and they had hooked ends similar to shepherd's crooks. Again broken and discarded now but yet again, something that today would probably command a reasonably high price as an example of the glass artisan's art.

The moral is that we seldom place a great deal of value on what we possess at any one time; not until many years later when their worth becomes more apparent. Was it ever thus?

At home, there was my mother Mary Anne Elizabeth, commonly known to her sisters by those initials as Mae, my father Benjamin, or Ben as he was known, brothers Jim and Dennis, sisters Edna and Beryl and me Brian William, or Bill as I tend to be called outside of the family; the baby of the family. It was a little crowded but we got by.

We tend to be a long-lived family; my father died in his eighties when I was 15 years old, my mother also in her eighties when I was in my early thirties. Edna the oldest sister (85), Beryl the second oldest (81) and Dennis the one before me (79) still survive. Only Jim has died though even he was in his seventies when he passed on, a victim of cancer. On the death of my mother, Edna became proxy mother and all family gatherings since then have tended to revolve around her, and to her I personally owe a great debt of gratitude that has lasted all my life. She has been my support, both financially and morally, in the way my life turned out as it did.

Jim was the black sheep of the family. He was dishonourably discharged from the army after deserting on a number of occasions before, finally being discharged. Eventually even the army gave up on him. In civilian life he was a persistent thief of a lesser nature. By this, I mean he did not break into people's homes and was not violent to other people. More likely, he would pick up someone else's coat when leaving a pub, or sell a TV set he had taken out on hire purchase, in order to have a few pounds in his pocket. In and out of jail for minor thefts almost the whole of his adult life following his army experiences, Jim was a lovable rogue whom no one could dislike for very long. You swore to yourself you would not give him another penny in assistance, but you did.

Beryl and Dennis both eventually married and left the area. Beryl married to Des, was off to the wealthier climes of the more affluent southern areas of Birmingham, while Dennis married Hazel who he met during his army service, and went off to Newark in Nottinghamshire, where he became a bus driver and, finally a bus inspector.

To the best of my recollection, my father was unemployed for the whole of my life until the day he died of stomach cancer when I was 15 years old. These days he would probably have lived longer and not have had to suffer the pain he did, but this was before the days of Macmillan cancer care and modern medicine. He was a man shorter in physical stature than I, being about 5 foot 8 inches tall, but he seemed almost as broad as he was tall. However, by the time the cancer had done with him, he was a shell of a man.

His long-term unemployment was not because of any wish to be idle but due to the fact he had very bad dermatitis in both legs. He had suffered this from his earlier work as a furnace man at the local gasworks. I suppose amongst some today he would be called a lay-about who avoided work. Under today's Coalition Government he would probably be told that as long as he could stand on two feet, he would be ineligible for support and should be out there working. You currently hear of many cases like that in today's media. Apparently, a body put in charge of assessing the ability of people to work by the current Coalition is doing a grand job in forcing people off the benefit list, despite their clear inability to work. What next, the workhouse? Come back Charles Dickens, you would recognise this world.

Could I be wrong, in my condemnation of the current Coalition government regarding welfare and the social conditions that currently exist? Maybe it is me that is interpreting these issues incorrectly, and that the government is adopting the correct approach to the so-called national financial problems. Why is it then that the former Archbishop of Canterbury, Dr Rowan Williams, has publicly condemned attitudes that ignore such things as food poverty, and the growth of food-banks, in what is still an affluent society. He is not alone in his approach to these problems, religious leaders across the spectrum have commented on the problems faced by large numbers of our fellow UK citizens. One of the said food-banks, the Tressel Trust, has alone provided sufficient food for a three day period to almost 750,000 people in 2013. They are not alone for such food-banks have proliferated in recent years. Even the more affluent areas of the country have been affected with, for instance, Dr Williams now becoming a patron for a Cambridge food-bank. Such food-banks have been doubling in number each year recently. Dr Williams is not alone for even the current Archbishop of Canterbury, Justin Welby, has endorsed the Bishops who have highlighted these problems.

Are religious leaders the only ones concerned with these problems? Doctors are now treating some of their patients for anxiety and depression, patients who often sit before them with their heads in their hands in "utter despair". Parents having to go without food themselves, in order that their children may have food to eat. Even parliament has, at last, recognised that a problem exists with the formation of an All Party Parliamentary Group on Hunger and Food Poverty. When will the party in power acknowledge that this situation exists and that "There are around six million working poor in the UK, people who are struggling to make ends meet in low paid or bitty employment" as Dr Williams has pointed out. Yet, the current government has apparently recently refused food aid from the European Union. Are members of the current government too proud to admit a problem exists?

Actually, given there was little financial support in those far off days of the 1940s and 1950s, for people like my father, he could hardly be called a scrounger, though certain groups in modern day society would perhaps fail to draw the distinction. Perhaps, in the modern era, he might even have been able to claim compensation for his industrial disability, which at that time he could not. However, despite his physical disability, he seemed a reasonably contented man who enjoyed his pipe and the radio and the odd pint of beer, while he sat by the fire in his rocking chair. Doctors seemed not to be able to cure his dermatitis and the only relief he obtained was from an ointment from the little grocer's shop in our street. I seem to recall this ointment was called Indian Syrite. After applying the ointment he wound bandages around his legs. Not sure about the spelling of Syrite but it was something akin to that. It was a long time ago!

My mother, therefore, was the principal wage earner until my older brothers and sisters went to work. During the day, she worked as a cook at a local grocer's shop. The shop owner had a fairly substantial shed erected in her back garden to cater for workers from several local factories. The factories are now long gone as manufacturing has declined, to be replaced by the service industries. The shop provided dinners, or what I suppose many would call lunches, though these were meat and three vegetable meals of some substance. Jam roly-roly or spotted dick with custard seemed to be the favourite desserts. On many occasions the potatoes that were prepared during the morning at our house were carried the half mile up to the shop by yours truly. I seem to remember they were carried up in an iron pot which seemed to weigh half a ton by the time I arrived at the shop. Not quite sure why this preparation took place at our house. Surely it would have made better sense to get them peeled at the shop? Perhaps the other members of staff at the shop were too busy preparing the other parts of the meals.

Meals were served over a two-hour period between 12 noon and 2pm, this straddled the normal one-hour dinner break periods for several local factories and these times allowing for several sittings. As noted above, none of those factories exist any longer, as a result of inept government policies in the 1960s, 70s and 80s. Nothing seems to have improved in the more recent era either. There seems to have been an inappropriate emphasis on financial services for the last thirty years, to the detriment of manufacturing in the UK. I wonder if anyone has noticed that the major economic power in Europe, Germany, bases its continued wealth and position in the world on making manufactured goods that the rest of the world wants! You will also note that, because Germany has not focused most of its attention on financial services, unlike the UK, it has escaped most of the impacts of the recent corruption associated with that segment of the economy, particularly in the Banking sector.

During the evenings, my mother also worked as an office cleaner at Evered's factory on Lewisham Road. This took from about 6pm until 10pm. In addition to all this, she took care of five kids and maintained our own home. All of this without any of the convenient utilities such as washing machines, refrigerators or dishwashers that exist today.

I guess, that the one simple pleasure she enjoyed was going up to the local pub, The Wagon and Horses on Lewisham Road, on Sunday lunchtime for a couple of drinks with her friends. I usually went as well and sat in the corridor outside the Assembly Room with a bottle of Vimto and a packet of crisps, my weekly treat. In addition to the large Assembly Room, there was the Smoking Room, a Gents Only room, a Saloon Bar-where my mother sat with her friends-and an off-license. These days I am not sure whether a 'Gents Only' room would be allowed, or even thought of, since it would be considered politically incorrect; maybe they could call it a Persons' Room!

By around 1.30pm, but certainly well before they called last orders, the coach which had taken the Wagon and Horses fishing fraternity on their early morning outing returned and they left their fishing baskets in the corridor. These baskets—creels—were osier baskets and they were left close to where I sat. The anglers specialised mostly in pike fishing and the fish they caught were laid out on top of their baskets to display them to the admiring populace. I recall that there was almost always at least one pike on each basket and usually they seemed to weigh in the region of 15 or 20lbs. One day I must go back to the Wagon and Horses to see how much it, and the fishermen, may have changed. Perhaps even the pub no longer exists and almost certainly, even if it is still there, whether the fishermen still partake in their sport is open to debate. Such social cohesion may have been totally lost?

There was a very long garden at 93 Sydenham Road in which vegetables were grown; potatoes, cabbages, carrots and leeks seemed to be the most popular. The back garden was also the site of our Anderson shelter, remember these were the early days of the war since I was born in 1938, the year that conflict broke out in Europe, but had yet to make a major impact in the UK. Dad also kept pigs at the bottom of the extended garden. Actually the pigsty was in an extension into what was a garage area running between our street and the next street over. I recall also that there was both a blackberry bush and a blackcurrent bush at the bottom of that garden which left your fingers and mouth purple when you had helped yourself to their fruit. Chickens were kept in the back yard in an extended chicken run. One of the consequences of the war was that the shortage of food led to the need for a degree of self sufficiency. And I recall that some of the produce tended to have to be shared with the local community, as called for by government dictate. The pigs in particular were taken away to be slaughtered and certain parts returned as our share. One year, my father managed to obtain a young turkey which was fed up for Christmas. To us kids it became a pet which was coddled and fed and looked after as a pet. Come Christmas dad wrung its neck and hung it up before it was prepared for Christmas dinner. He and my mother tucked into it with relish, but I do not think many of us kids could bear to touch it.

What did Christmas hold in store for a young lad like me? Well my Christmas stocking was just that, one of my sisters-usually laddered-stockings. What was it filled with? Perhaps an orange and some nuts, plus a few pennies or the odd sixpence, and some sweets. Maybe a couple of comic annuals and a few crayons or coloured pencils, plus a few other bits and pieces. Nothing much really, but then we did not have very much.

As an aside regarding that long garden at number 93, it was where I almost killed a playmate! A neighbour who had spent time in Africa had brought back to the UK many souvenirs of his stay there, including elephant ear shields, strings of ornate shells and throwing spears. My pal Martin and I were chasing each other around the garden and I playfully threw one of the spears. It sailed through the air and thudded down to the ground. Martin screamed and stood stock still looking down. The spear had gone through his plimsoll and pinned his foot to the ground. Fortunately, it had only struck him between his big toe and the adjacent one, slightly nicking the web between them. Safe to say, the spears were taken away and never seen again.

There was no bathroom in our house and, usually during my earlier years, on Friday nights a tin bath that hung on a hook outside the back door was brought in for my weekly bath, in front of that religiously black-leaded fire. Later on, when I was about ten or eleven years old, I went down to Rolfe Street Baths for my weekly bath. It was quite a luxury to laze in a hot bath for a half hour, at least I think you were allowed half an hour. At Rolfe Street they had a series of individual rooms equipped with the usual four legged iron baths. If memory serves me well, I believe it cost sixpence in old money and, for this, they provided a towel and a small piece of soap. Maybe this early deprivation, of tin baths in front of the fire at home, and iron baths at Rolfe Street, is the cause of my obsession with early morning showers each day!

Alongside the bath on the back wall of the house there was a washing tub and dolly which my mother used to wash clothes and, alongside that the wringer that squeezed out most of the water from the wet clothes, before they were hung on the washing line. The hot water needed for the wash was heated in the iron boiler that occupied one corner of the kitchen and was, in turn heated by a coal fire underneath.

Since there was no bathroom or indoor toilet at our house we were obliged, even on the coldest, wettest and iciest nights, to step out into the backyard to the toilet. It was situated between the coal shed and a storage shed in which, I seem to recall, brother Dennis at one time kept pigeons. On the opposite side of the backyard was the chicken run, housing mainly Rhode Island Red chickens. My father swore they produced bigger and tastier eggs than any other breed, though he also had a breed which I think was called a Leghorn.

Since my father seldom left the house, other than to look after the animals or work in the garden, his one pleasure seemed to be a couple of pints of beer which I was obliged to fetch from the local off license at the top of our street. A dark brown quart bottle was hefted up the road to be filled by the local publican, not sure if it's correct to call an off license owner a publican. He had a copper funnel which he stuck into the bottle and then pulled on the beer pump handle until the bottle was full. I seem to think it cost just a few pence for a quart of beer.

As mentioned earlier, Dad had two other vices, his pipe being one. He smoked something called 'twist'. It was like a stick of liquorice from which he cut a piece and then rubbed this between the balls of his hands to shred it until he could fill his pipe. He then sat there, by the side of the fire in his rocking chair, contentedly puffing away on his pipe and usually listening to the radio. The other small pleasure he enjoyed was an occasional dabble on the horses. Our radio, like many others at the time, was run on square glass rechargeable batteries. When these needed recharging I had to take them up to a man two streets away, who refilled them with distilled water and recharged them. Why did they have to be recharged somewhere else? Because our house was lit by gas, fragile little gas mantles that broke if you were too clumsy in lighting them with a match or a paper spill, no electricity for us as that time.

The two items, batteries and betting, came together for this battery man doubled as the, illegal at that time, local bookie. A slip of paper with Dad's selections was handed over at the same time as the batteries for charging. Dad seldom won but the bet was just for a few pence, certainly less than a shilling. This provided him with a little harmless pleasure, waiting to find out the results in tomorrow's paper, usually the Daily Mirror as I recall, and he perhaps had a few shillings in return, which was collected by me when picking up the recharged batteries. Occasionally, when he won, I received a few pence of my own to spend.

I guess that throughout my life, my taste for gambling was one of the main things that I inherited from my father; I am my father's son. I have always enjoyed taking on the bookmakers and, in the following pages, I relate a few of the more successful ventures into the bookmaker's domain. I am not a great one for the greyhounds, though there was one instance where I more than dipped my toe in the water even there, but that story is for a little later in this odyssey. As noted, you will find this story peppered with tales of successful betting, on the horses, after all, who wants to remember the failures, of which there were many.

Only once in my lifetime as a youngster did my father hit me; that was in about 1947 and, on reflection, I had been inconsiderate, though I was still a nine-year-old kid who just did not think. Together with several other lads, we went straight from school down to an area we called the Lanes but which was more formally called Wosson, an area of countryside bordering between Smethwick, West Bromwich and Birmingham. The Jubilee coal mine was there in Wosson and the drainage from it had created a small lake—the source of our interest because of the frogs and newts that it attracted. Wosson was also where the military Tanks manufactured half a mile away at the Birmingham Carriage Works had been taken to be tested in the water dip and in other areas of the Lanes during the war years. On this one occasion, we went frog spawning. A few jam jars and there it was long strings of frog spawn which we collected and eventually wending our way home at about 9pm that warm summer's evening, jars full of frog spawn. The old man stood at the back gate. He took the jar off me and threw it in the hole that had been left by the dismantling of our Anderson shelter and which was partially filled with rain water since the hole had not yet been filled in, then he smacked me around the ears. *"That's for worrying your mother for not knowing where you were. Never ever do that again"*

I'm not sure if any of the other lads who went frog spawning with me were treated in a similar fashion. I did not tell them what happened to me and they did not tell me about their welcome home. I would guess they were similarly admonished but none of us confessed to each other. I guess pride was a factor even then. I never did cause my mother similar problems ever again. Maybe there is a lesson in this to be learnt by modern parents, though I imagine being prosecuted for child abuse given modern day political correctness might prevail. However, some days later our garden and all those around us were inundated by a plague of tiny frogs. Like me, they had developed and survived!

After that, whenever the other lads and I went down to Wosson it was always after telling everyone where we were going. Usually our journeys were during the summer time when there were long sunny days and evenings and these visits were usually associated with looking for birds' eggs. Yes, I know its not considered proper these days, but it was one of the few ways of entertaining ourselves in those days when adults as well as children were obliged to seek entertainment where it could be found. It was a wonderful way to spend a hot summer's day. We were, however, conscious of not taking all the eggs from a nest; one per nest was the rule. We carried match boxes or little tin boxes into which we had put plucked grass—I still cannot smell freshly cut grass without thinking of those outings. Sometimes if we had been thinking a bit forward we had put in a bit of cotton wool or a bit of soft cloth in our boxes. We would put the egg into the box to protect it until we returned home; there, we inserted a pin into each end of the egg and blew out the contents. Half the pleasure we got from egg collecting was in looking at the fantastic colour's, and sizes and shapes of the different eggs: sky blues, deep mottled browns, speckled greens and almost pure whites. There were tiny finch eggs and the larger starlings and thrushes eggs, maybe a plovers if we had a lucky find.

I remember that on these excursions down Wosson there was a natural spring and that, when the weather was really hot during those early summers, nothing tasted as good as the cold water bubbling up from below the ground as we cupped our hands and drank. My mouth waters at the thought of it, even now.

Such simple pleasures which I doubt many children can indulge in these days, given the almost obsessive degree of protection that takes place against threat's imagined, or considered to be, a danger to their well-being. Maybe one of the reasons why modern children suffer from asthma and other similar diseases is that they are not exposed to germs and the environment in the natural way that we were in those far off days. Because food was at a premium for children such as us, if we dropped a jam buttie (sandwich) in the street we picked it up and ate it. What is that saying about eating a peck of dirt during your lifetime? It can't have been too bad for us since I can confirm that I have never spent a night in hospital through ill health, other than for an eye operation at the age of 14.

One of my other real pleasures at that time was the local cinema, the Beacon on Brasshouse Lane. From a quite young age, I was there every Saturday morning for the kids' matinee. Flash Gordon and the evil Ming, Tom Mix, Roy Rogers and Hopalong Cassidy—these were the escape from reality for us since clearly, in our circle, there was no TV at that time. I also remember, once or twice, visiting one of the Smethwick cinemas with my mother. I think it was the Empire, which put on variety shows several times a month—something I think Americans call 'burlesque' and, sadly, a thing of the past. Usually, there were magicians, jugglers, singers and dancers, with the odd comedian thrown in.

There was also the radio. Tommy Handley, Workers' Playtime, Ben Lyon and Bebe Daniels, Dick Barton Special Agent with Jock and Snowy, and of course, that most ridiculous radio programme of all time, Peter Brough and Archie Andrews—a ventriloquist on radio! You certainly could not see Peter Brough's lips move.

Later on, as a young teenager, I was probably up at the Beacon cinema or down on Smethwick High Street at the Princess cinema, at least twice a week. Sometimes, this involved having to ask an adult who was going in if I could go in with them because an 'A' film was on. As a youngster, you were not allowed to go in on your own for these 'A' film's, you had to be accompanied by an adult. Good grief, these day's people would have palpitations at the thought of kids going into a cinema with an unknown adult. Such is the loss of innocence. Occasionally there was a horror film, or what was alluded to as an 'adult film' and, here, you certainly had to be accompanied by an adult. In general, the horror films were quite rubbishy and the adult films never did actually show anything that could be called corrupting of youth. The same cannot be said for the cinema or the TV of today, as it seems as though anything goes; though, again, it's a question of degree and the individual's perceptions. Good job I am not a prude, although during this little essay I probably come across as one, or there would be nothing for me to watch.

However, one film in particular sticks in my mind and this one did make a shiver run down my spine at that young age. I was probably about 10 or 11 years old, and managed to get into the Princess cinema, accompanied by an adult who I managed to persuade to take me in. I believe it was Boris Karloff in the starring role and the film was called 'The Mummy's Hand'. At one point in the film a group of actors in a pyramid and, of course, filmed in the dark with flickering candlelight, were starting to open a coffin and as they began to lean forward, eager to see the contents a hand shot out of the coffin and grabbed one of them by the throat. Half the audience shot out of their seats and I spent the best part of the rest of the film with my face very close to the seat in front. These days, kids of 10 or 11 seem to watch people being cut up and slashed as though it's the commonest thing in the world. Gory video games seem to be the most popular things they can get their hands on, I know, I have a great nephew who seems to be addicted to them.

As we grew a little older, maybe 13 or 14 years old, a bunch of us lads jumped on our bikes and cycled to places like Bewdley or Stourport. It was about 20 miles, as I recall, but there was far less traffic on the roads and riding a bicycle at that time was a far more pleasurable pursuit than it is today. Cycling in the UK, as an adult, has now become a real hazard and I have the feeling that cyclists' are treated merely as targets by some drivers. The statistics on cyclists' deaths seem to bear this out since last year dozens of cyclists were killed on the road by motor vehicles. I know it almost breaks the hearts of all those motorists who say cyclists' are a nuisance, and should be paying taxes to use the roads. Is this a good reason to drive them into the gutters or even drive over them? Remember, you are driving a vehicle weighing far more than your target and capable of bringing serious injury and death to another human being. Does that ring a bell in your consciousness?

On one occasion when, as an adult and living in Brighton, a double-decker bus drove me into the gutter, I noticed him hitting the kerb a little further down the road. I hope the driver was surprised when he arrived at his garage to find I had telephoned from my office to inform them that they had a driver on that service who was either drunk or on drugs! Incidentally, I received no confirmation of any action taken by the bus company against that driver. I am not too surprised by that failure to respond; these days dealing with the public for some companies seems too much of a bother. Public relations, what on earth is that? By the way I am a cyclist, motor cyclist and car driver myself and always practice what I preach regarding the safety of other road users. God, here I go again, doing the 'nose in the air stuff'.

I was taught to drive by a day release prisoner from Winson Green prison in Birmingham, by the way. He informed me that he was a get-away driver for a gang of bank robbers. I suspect he was just a con man. However, he was an excellent driving instructor and I still drive in the way he stressed; for example always indicate well in advance of turning, even when there is no other vehicle behind you. He said, *"If you do this when you do not need to, you will not forget it when you do need to, and always use your mirrors when changing direction".*

At the bottom of Brasshouse Lane and near to Smethwick High Street there was the railway line of the London Midland and Scottish Railway (LMS). Not far away, near Spon Lane, there was the Great Western line (GWR). This, of course, was at the time of steam trains; at that time, diesel and electric trains were mostly something for the future. It seems to me that, in modern times, the railways are purely functional and not such an efficient method of getting from A to B, what with crowded trains and late arrivals. Yet again, the term 'public service' seems to have become a forgotten word since the 'services' were privatised. In those earlier days, with steam trains and something called British Rail, there was a hint of what I suppose could be called romance and adventure? I had two little books which contained all the train numbers and names, both passenger and freight, one for the LMS service and one for the GWR. I would sit for hours watching the trains go by and feeling great when a named train—the Castles, the Lords, the Abbeys, went flashing past. A simple pleasure that would be called 'geeky' in today's rather more cynical world.

Smethwick, at that time, was one of the most heavily industrialised towns in the Midlands, if not the country. There were miles of canals that had in earlier years supplied the factories and foundries with their raw materials for work: building materials, coal, metals, components and so on. And, as noted above, there was a network of railway lines and stations that serviced the whole area. Sited on the outskirts of Birmingham, Smethwick provided supplies, both components and materials, for even bigger concerns and also the necessary manual labour to feed the factories. Now, with the demise of so many industrial sites, Smethwick suffers with many other towns and cities from fairly serious industrial decline.

What has replaced the skills that abounded around the Birmingham area and its surrounding towns, at one time nicknamed the workshop of the world? Now there was employment in supermarkets, offices and shops. I guess that, now, people with power and influence prefer to use their money to create more money via financial services and to keep their hands relatively 'clean'. Whatever happened to families such as the Cadburys, and the Chamberlain's of yesteryear, who at least seemed to have a local social conscience to go with their commercial enterprises? The demise of manufacturing seemed, in later years, to be almost a conscious policy of certain governments. Were the workers in these industries seen as too challenging and threatening? Certainly, Maggie's war on the trade union's, and the miners in particular, seems to reflect this. Is it too different today, with the poorest members of society seeming to be bearing the brunt of economic pressures while the wealthier seem to get their taxes cut? Is it too difficult to comprehend that having a skilled, competent and committed workforce is a plus for a major developed nation? Are there no examples out there to show that a consensus relationship between employer, employee and the State is the way forward?

Of course there are! As noted above, Sweden, Germany and Japan spring to mind straight away. In the UK however, ever since the beginning of the industrial revolution relations between employer and labour have been confrontational, and this has largely been the fault of the employers for not attempting to adopt consensus approaches and bring labour along with them, as evidenced in so many other countries. Strangely enough, this can be said of most of the English speaking world. Maybe the migration of people from the UK to what was then the Empire, and subsequently the Commonwealth, also spread this way of dealing with industrial relations, or non-relations as it could be called. Most of the non-English speaking industrialised nations seem to have gone for a much more consensus-based approach to manufacturing and to their employees, to their advantage. Not only do we seem to have created a workplace environment of confrontation for ourselves in the UK but also for much of the rest of the English speaking world!

It's interesting to note that the ex-Deputy Chief Constable of Manchester, John Stalker, has stated that, at the time of Margaret Thatcher's reign, those times were the closest the UK has reached towards becoming a police state, when a potentially politicised police force was used to prevent people crossing borders between counties, in an effort to stop strikers and their supporters from acting peacefully in concert. Whatever happened to the concept of mutual collaboration in a democratic society?

Why did some of the police, who were making a great deal of extra money from overtime work, consider it appropriate to wave their wage packet slips in the faces of the striking miners? It seems that provocation was something that some foolish people were unable to resist. Similarly, under recent disclosures it appears that up to 4,500 army personnel were put on standby by the then government to become lorry drivers to deliver coal around the country. Again, a provocative act. Taking industrial action is not illegal, or at least it was not then. Now it seems that most of the problems that existed at that time were down to the Unions and

that employers and government were blameless—or
that is what they would have you believe.

But back to earlier matters in my life: of course, it
was still war time when I was only a lad and food was
fairly limited in quality and quantity. But there was
initiative to be displayed and when a pig's head became
available it was simmered in the copper for hours until
the flesh peeled off easily and was placed in a white
crockery pudding basin with a saucer on top. The
meat was held in place by a good old fashioned metal
iron—none of your modern steam irons in those days.
A day or so later, when the flesh had become pressed
into Braun this was delicious on slices of fresh baked
bread which had been produced in that old black
living room fireplace oven. Then there were what was
called pigeon peas. These were known as 'grey peas'
for some reason, and were hard as nails, but actually
dark brown in colour. Soaked for hours in water, then
simmered for hours more, they then had added a little
salt and bits of bacon fat. Just thinking of them I can
still taste them now, so many years later.

Also, I seem to recall that the parts of animals that
did seem to be readily available and apparently
did not come under the rationing umbrella was
what are termed 'offal': kidneys, heart, and liver. In
modern days, some people might consider these as

inappropriate and beneath their dignity to eat. To us, they were a readily available source of food and nutrition. When my mother could get a beef heart, it was simmered very slowly until it became very tender and I defy any hungry child from enjoying it with his or her dinner. Cordon bleu cooking it was not but it fed us and I understand that, rather belatedly, it has been recognised that the diet during those war years was probably healthier than that currently enjoyed! And my old lady, my mom, was a very good cook. Yes, I know some of those foods noted above may sound distasteful to some of those who read this, but that was then and under the conditions that existed then. It was a question of using whatever was available, and nutritious and filling.

Today, options are far wider than most of the meals mentioned above, including fresh produce from all over the world. No longer do these earlier options, such as pig's heads and pigeon peas, exist for the majority of people. I suspect that, for those at the bottom of the economic pile today, similar meals have been replaced by cheap convenience foods that are inferior to the ones we consumed and are far less nutritious. In fact, I suspect, that far from being good for us, they are just the opposite. Certainly given the latest revelations of contaminated foodstuffs, they either seem often to contain elements not shown on the label or to have additives that may prove to be harmful in the long-term. Would I swap my earlier diet for a burger or a cheap packet of something that had been frozen and had to be put in the microwave for two minutes? No way.

As a war time youngster, I can only remember one instance when bombs were dropped nearby but there must have been more than that one occasion. Maybe I have blocked out other instances. I do remember going around with my pals, trying to finding bits of shrapnel in the streets around where we lived. The one bomb I do remember dropped one street away and I recall the whistling noise as it came down as we lay in the Anderson Shelter.

These bombs were aimed at the Birmingham Carriage Works which, before the war, had made railway carriages but now made the military tanks mentioned earlier. It fell midway between the Carriage works which were a few hundred yards away, and our home. I believe that the Germans failed to hit the carriage works substantially throughout that time though my memories may be wrong since it was quite a large sized manufacturing enterprise.

It seems that many of the people you speak to today have very clear recollections of their childhood. Some talk of remembering starting to walk, or talk, or going on holiday to the seaside when they were 1 or 2 years old. My earliest recollections are of when I was 4 years old and it was of a particular day. It was the day another child threw a handful of sand and grit into my face. My eyes were open and took the full force. I am told that it took four days to get me to open my eyes again. The eyes that had previously been a perfectly normal pair of hazel-coloured eyes were turned inwards, looking more at my nose than the world ahead. At the time I do not remember being particularly concerned, but it meant years of hospital visits trying to correct the squint that I had in both eyes.

A popular expression at the time—not so sure about modern days since it may be considered politically incorrect—was that I was 'bunk-eyed'. A cross-eyed geek. It seems, and I don't know how true this is, that the rubbish had got behind the eyes and had touched the optic nerves. What followed was ten years of twice weekly visits to Birmingham Eye Hospital for remedial treatment. This mostly comprised of a little machine where you put your chin on a support and gazed into two lenses. In one lit frame there was a monkey, in the other a cage. You manipulated the handles to try to get the monkey into the cage. There were other variations on the theme but this is the one that has remained in my mind. Another element of the treatment was to have one lens of my spectacles covered by sticky tape which was picked up on by my schoolmates. 'Specky one eye' became a new name for me.

The treatments worked pretty well for the right eye—not perfect but quite close—but not for the left eye. At the age of 14 I entered the Birmingham Eye hospital for corrective surgery. I remember the nurse telling me to keep my head quite still after surgery to allow the eye to heal completely and, for several days, I was a rock until the bandages were removed. That was the only time in my whole life that I have spent time laid up in Hospital. Fingers crossed! However, as a result of the dirt thrown into my face—I have spent a lifetime wearing spectacles.

As a consequence of the eye incident, for over ten years I had what could be termed a limited education, losing two days (40 per cent) out of each school week travelling to and from to the Birmingham Eye Hospital and receiving treatment, instead of the time I should have been attending school. By the way, this usually meant my mother being obliged to accompany me and that added yet more to her workload. This was during, and just after the war, and was from 1942 until just before I left school in 1953. You may recall that many of our finest young men and women were at that time otherwise engaged in something more immediate than education in the academic sense, though they were learning perhaps more important lessons.

Maybe the most memorable event during my early schooling, other than the eye event, occurred at the age of 7. That was VE day, Victory in Europe. The war in Europe had been won and the whole street celebrated. People who lived at one end of the street, and who perhaps had hardly ever spoken to people from the other end of the street, all came together contributing whatever they had to the street party. Flags and buntings ran from lamp post to lamp post. Tables were laid down half the length of the street, covered by fresh tablecloths. There was jelly and blancmange, fish-paste sandwiches and freshly baked cakes. Although food was still rationed everyone contributed what they could.

After the party, when the tables had been cleared away, the kids in the street took turns to be given rides around the block by Cyril Evans in his little car—a real novelty in those days for us kids. This was an event I remember quite clearly since when it came to my turn and I climbed into the back seat, I had my hand around the central column between the front and rear open doors. Result: one slammed door, one smashed finger nail which eventually blackened and fell off. I still have the crescent-shaped mark in that finger nail to remind me of the occasion.

In the evening, and once the party was over and the tables were cleared away, stacks of wood which had been collected and stored in back gardens were carried out into the street and a huge bonfire was built. It burnt through the tarred and pebbled road surface and the aftermath was visible for many months afterwards until the road was resurfaced. There were a few fireworks available and sparklers. Potatoes and chestnuts were roasted and the party went on till the early hours of the following day.

Having mentioned Cyril Evans, I should note that he, together with his brother Harold, owned the one business in the street apart from a coal merchant's near the corner with Lewisham Road, and the little shop across the street. His business produced boiled beetroot, though perhaps steamed would be more accurate, this was for local markets, particularly in Birmingham. There was the boiler and a packing shed and that was about it. The boiled beetroots had the skins peeled off them by hand, which was quite easy to do once they had been boiled. Then, when they had cooled, over to the packing shed where my sisters worked for a while, wrapping them in cellophane and placing them in boxes, and where I also earned a few shillings for helping out. The beetroot was loaded into a flat-back lorry and sent off to market.

Cyril and Harold were also grass track motorcycle racers. On Sunday mornings, they loaded their motorcycle and sidecar onto the same truck used for distributing the beetroot and off they went to different tracks around the Midlands to compete. Occasionally, I was on the back of the lorry with the bike and enjoyed those days out.

The more normal forms of entertainment for us kids in those early years usually comprised of playing French cricket in the street or football shots-in against a wall at the corner of the street. I guess that, if you tried it these days you would probably be knocked over by the traffic or arrested for causing a nuisance. I can't remember the last time I saw kids playing in the street like this. Personally, I am glad to be the age I am at the moment, I would hate to be young these days. Everything seems so much less free and happy. Fear and selfishness seem to prevail, or is that the misperception of an old man?

I remember one Saturday afternoon when I was about 5 or 6 years old, I was on my own and kicking a tennis ball against the wall at the front of our house when the Albion crowd of supporters came streaming down our street after the Saturday afternoon game had finished. We only lived about half a mile from the Hawthorns, the West Bromwich Albion football ground. One passing chap said *"Use your left foot son the Baggies are looking for someone with a left foot"*. I immediately switched to my left foot and, who knows, it might have been that which helped turn me into a half decent footballer. More of that later but, when I was only a little older paying sixpence to go to a match myself was a real treat. Once a Baggie, always a Baggie.

There are a couple of Albion games that I attended much later that spring to mind, and perhaps this is the spot to note them before moving on. The first was a match against what were known as the Manchester United 'Busby Babes'. Probably one of the best matches ever between these two long established football clubs, both of whom were noted for playing good football. Albion won 4-3. The reason why this sticks in the mind is that it was not long afterwards that there occurred the disastrous Munich aircraft crash which killed many members of that wonderful United team. One of those to lose his life was the magnificent Duncan Edwards, a Black Country lad from over Dudley way who had earlier become one of the youngest ever England international footballers.

Another Albion match that I attended, was of a testimonial match for Norman Heath the West Bromwich goalkeeper who was seriously injured in a match up at Sunderland. Over 40,000 people attended the match against a team composed, at that time, of past and present international footballers. That match was kicked off by a TV celebrity by the name of Sabrina. Sabrina was a lady of ample proportions, much in the mould of Diana Dors. She was driven around the pitch in an open topped American Cadillac, sitting up on top of the back seat shortly before the kick-off, much to the delight of the supporters.

My two favourite players at the Albion played for them a long time ago. Ronnie Allen, a goal scoring genius who set up as many goals for his colleagues, particularly Johnny Nicholls and Derek Kevan, as he scored for himself. One season Ronnie and Johnny, knocked up almost seventy goals between them. However, my favourite player of all time was the elegant Ray Barlow a midfield passer of the ball that would have made David Beckham envious. He could place the ball on a sixpence with either foot. Sadly Ray died quite recently.

Sorry for the diversion, back to my childhood and another childish game at that time was knocking on people's doors in the dark evenings and then running and hiding. Such simple pleasures, until I ran straight into the local policeman who slapped me around the ears and told me to go home. By the way, once again I did not tell anyone at home what had happened—perhaps out of pride, who knows. Today it would probably be called police brutality!

Football or proper forms of cricket were played in the local Lewisham Road Park about half a mile away and opposite the Birmingham and Midlands Aluminium Works, or Birmid as it was called for short. Being one of the older kids in our little gang I, along with Roy W, who was a similar age and lived across the road from our house (and who incidentally may have been the assailant in the eye attack) were usually the captains. Any kids standing around in the park were allowed to join in, each one being added sequentially to the two teams to maintain parity. The goal posts were formed by our pullovers or coats and there was endless debate about whether a particular shot was too high to be a goal or not. These football games were fought with great intensity and over a long period, usually resulting in something like 27:23 score lines. I guess that was to be expected when games could take three hours or more and have about fifteen players per side. You know, maybe my memory is failing but I can't remember ever hearing any of those kids swear, or dive, or pretend to be injured in the way that modern kids do when they ape their elders. Modern professional footballers have a lot to answer for, regarding the attitudes and activities of modern youngsters.

For most of my early formal education I was taught by somewhat older people than would have been the norm in other times, perhaps by individuals who had formally retired and had been brought back into teaching to fill the gap left by those younger persons, now serving in the armed forces. Maybe some of these people did not have the energy or desire to be there any longer. This is not to disparage the many fine teachers who soldiered on, but perhaps we might have had more committed teachers if they had not been engaged in the war effort.

You may already have discovered my lack of more formal and precise grammar. We were not taught the niceties of the English language and, despite that fact, I have since produced numerous articles and chapters in books, and been responsible for editing various publications, I still do not know what a split infinitive is, nor do I feel the slightest guilt about this.

Many years after leaving school and working in academia, I submitted a paper to a refereed journal. I think the journal may have been *Omega*. The article was accepted but the publisher sent me a copy of one of the reviews. It was by a famous and respected writer of left wing leanings, with considerable knowledge of the subject I had covered and, on which I was publishing previously unknown data. I am kind of left wing myself, not to too great a degree but I feel more comfortable with that side of the political spectrum. However, this review did surprise me somewhat. Almost all of the critique was about the written English, with nothing about the technical aspects of the research I was reporting upon. It made me realise that pedants can come from all sides of the political spectrum. Was there nothing technical in the article that he considered worthy of comment? Perhaps he was annoyed that he had not done that piece of research himself? I have to confess that I have found, through considerable exposure to the academic world later in my life, that there is nothing as self-serving as many senior academics.

On another occasion, a book for which I had been the sole editor ended up with three supposed editors. It is the convention in academia that, with one or two authors or editors, both are mentioned when it is being referenced. With three or more authors or editors however, it is the senior author/editor who is cited with a simple 'et al;' for the others. In this instance although he had contributed almost nothing to the volume, the Professor concerned become the prime editor and consigned myself to being a footnote! Incidentally, the third so-called editor had died several months prior to the book being edited! In later years, when I co-authored articles with others, I made sure that even my research assistant became the first author when they had contributed most to the paper.

Although I cannot claim great literacy, for me words are there to explain a situation, to inform, or to be informed by. Actually, I have always thought I write conversationally more than anything else. I like to exchange ideas via the written word and to conduct a conversation with the reader. More about my publications later, if you have the patience and/or desire to continue, though I must say that, actually, a colleague once commented that I wrote in the style of someone from the last century, by which he meant the nineteenth century!

From the age of 5 to 7 I attended Brasshouse Lane Infant School in, where else would it be, Brasshouse Lane. Of two clear images that have lasted me a lifetime the first is of the free milk we received every day. What a luxury and, Oh Maggie, why did you have to go and do it? Well we know why she did it and its still inexcusable. For a good part of the population, the nickname 'Maggie Thatcher, milk snatcher' seemed most appropriate. If ever a politician attracted equal measures of approbation and revulsion, it was her. Her advocates were, and still are, passionate in her defence while people like me derided her. My opinion of her has not mellowed with age. Current studies have shown that a glass of milk, or should I say a little bottle of milk which was what we received every day, was a very beneficial health supplement at that time and still considered so today, though others claim otherwise. Why is it that, whatever food or drink we consume these days, there is always a debate about it: whether it is good for you or not? For example, dairy products such as butter, milk and cheese will lead you to an early grave, according to some people, yet are considered essential for good health by others! By the way, I consume plenty of all three but am still alive at the age of 75 and still reasonably active, both physically and mentally.

The second infant school image I retain was an agony to me. At the tender age of 6 I was hauled up onto the stage for morning assembly in front of the whole school, by the headmistress. My sin? I had completed a math's paper of twenty questions and they were all correct, with a gold star to boot. I was mortified by having to stand up there and never achieved the same result again in mathematics. Was the earlier result a fluke or was the decline in achievement intended to avoid the humiliation I felt? I still do not know, but I think it was the latter.

After the infants school, in 1945, it was off across the road to Brasshouse Lane Junior School. My main memories here are of walls painted a shiny dark green, and floors painted a similarly shiny, but this time dark red: winding staircases in a Victorian building, morning assembly with singing and morning prayers. Of the education, I can recall virtually nothing other than the opportunity to play football on the school sports field which was several hundred yards down the road and on the opposite side of the street.

Do all schools still have sports fields? I somehow doubt it, since current government policy seems to be to make schools sell off everything not tied down in order to maintain the rest of the school because State funds have been cut back or withdrawn. Maybe this is so they can save some money to pay their own inflated salaries or provide sustenance for their wealthier friends? The cynic emerges yet again! Yes, despite attempts to say the class system is dead, this is far from the truth. Funny how the people making these decisions affecting people lower down the social scale do not have to rely on State facilities since they are normally quite wealthy. Many are millionaires from privileged backgrounds who are educating their own children in private schools with plenty of sports facilities. I believe something like half of the current Coalition government Cabinet members are actually millionaires several times over. If the above sounds too class conscious to some of you I make no apologies for this. Anyone who cares to read newspapers, or watch television news or social documentary programmes these days has to be extremely aware that many thousands, if not millions of UK citizens are deeply aware of the social divisions that surround us.

Both of the schools in Brasshouse Lane have now been demolished and other buildings erected in their place. I believe they are mostly residential though I have not been back to the area for many years. Certainly, the old football pitch has gone and the area is now occupied by houses and flats.

I have to confess I was never a good dedicated pupil while at school either at the infants, the juniors, or finally the Secondary Modern school I attended. So in 1949 and at the age of eleven it was off to senior school. This was about two miles away and was in the fairly modern buildings of Smethwick Hall Secondary Modern in Stoney Lane. Again, it seemed all you had to do was sort of amble along from classroom to classroom: no pressure, no inclination to be pushed to achieve. Disinterest seemed to be the prevailing mood and that was as much from the teachers as it was from us pupils.

Some days, I was able to catch the bus to school which cost a couple of pence on the Midland Red service but on other days, it was about a two mile walk. It did not seem too onerous however at that time, and time seemed to drift by. I still recall the route. Down Sydenham Road, across Lewisham Road, along Kimberley Road, down Brasshouse Lane, over the railway bridge and on to Smethwick High Street, across to Stoney Lane and after about half a mile or so, there was the school up a gentle slope on the right and on top of the rise, looking down on all it surveyed. Behind the school, there were the playing fields, ergo football pitches.

The one redeeming factor at Smethwick Hall was, again, football. I was pretty good at it and games periods were my saving grace. At that time, football boots were made of quite thick leather and had high sides to protect the ankles. After every game, it was a case of scraping off the mud that had accumulated around the studs and applying dubbin, a light coloured greasy substance, to try to soften and maintain the stiff leather. If a stud had been lost, you just nailed another one on and hammered it in hoping the nails did not go through and stick up inside the boot. In that case you had to hammer them flat from the inside so they did not stick into the bottom of your foot.

Other than football my years at Smethwick Hall passed in a haze. I have few memories of either the teachers or my fellow students and cannot remember other than one single name. That name was Dickie D. Dickie D was the science teacher even then an elderly man and even then what I would now call morose. I recall little of what he taught. He is remembered because of his accuracy at hurling the blackboard rubber. This was a piece of wood with a felt insert. If anyone dared to talk in class, he would throw this with incredible accuracy at the offending student. How anyone can identify a particular child when the teacher had his back turned to the class I do not know, but Dickie D could.

It was perhaps no surprise to anyone, myself included, when at the age of 15 and on leaving school, I did so with no paper qualifications and drifted into unskilled employment.

Early Employment

Unlike today, at that time in 1953, it was fairly easy to get a job though, without qualifications nothing too exotic. For me, it was Phillips Cycles factory in Bridge Street, about half a mile away from home and quite close to the local canal where lunch time football became the order of the day. The factory was where I became what could be described as a piece of human machine-fodder. Right up until I was conscripted into the RAF at the age of 18, I spent my time either sticking bits of metal into machines, using hand presses joining one bit of metal to another bit of metal, or drilling holes in bits of metal, either at Phillips Cycles or at the aforementioned Birmid factory.

At the age of 15, for a 40-hour working week, I earned £1 2s 6p for manipulating those bits of metal in a machine. Actually, the bit of metal at Phillips was the central spindle that runs through the centre of the pedal and attaches the pedal to the bicycle. After a while, I graduated to piece-work on the hand presses and could earn a little more money but it was still a depressingly boring job and time lumbered on. Of course, Phillips Cycles no longer exists in Smethwick a result of the demise of much of Britain's, and certainly Smethwick's manufacturing base.

However, there was one major plus to working for Phillips Cycles: they had a football team playing in the Birmingham Works Youth League and I played for them. We were pretty good and only Accles and Pollocks over in Oldbury were a slightly better and slightly more successful team. The two teams always finished first and second in the league, with us usually second, but I recall we had a better Cup record and usually managed to win those games.

Of the eleven regulars in our team, ten were on the books of either, Aston Villa, Birmingham, Wolverhampton, or the Albion. I was the exception. I was booked for a trial but, on the Saturday prior to the trial, while playing for Phillips, I twisted my back badly playing on a mud heap of a pitch which was quite cloying. My studs had stuck in the muddy pitch and, as I tried to turn quickly I badly wrenched my back. Within minutes, I was dragging my left leg and had to leave the pitch. A few minutes after the accident I was in agony and I could hardly walk. I was placed in an ambulance and taken off to Dudley Road hospital in Birmingham, now I believe it's called City

Hospital. There I was encased with a plaster of paris cast which I had to endure for six weeks. The cast encircled my waist and was fitted from just below my ribs down to my groin, not a pleasant thing to come to terms with. For the following six weeks I was pretty well totally incapacitated, barely able to bend or twist my body. Sleeping with this cast on was a nightmare.

After the cast was removed there was a period of six weeks of physiotherapy, massage and heat treatment at the hospital to get some mobility back and, get off the extra 10lbs of weight I had put on while compelled to live a more or less sedentary lifestyle. However, my chance of a trial with one of the local clubs had gone and within just a few months my call up to the armed forces beckoned for two years. Of course, having a trial with a professional football club these days at the age of 16 or 17 would be almost unimaginable since teams now focus on 7 or 8 year olds to develop at their in-house academies.

Ever since starting work at Phillips Cycles, and playing football for them, I had been training five nights a week under the guidance of an ex-West Bromwich Albion and England full back, Cecil Shaw. Even though in his 60s I think Cecil was probably fitter than us youngsters and was as hard as nails. In addition to matches, we had stamina running over several miles and some innovative training methods, which included learning to play tennis to increase mobility and flexibility. The football accident turned me from an extremely fit 17 year old who had been playing football twice a week, once for Phillips on Saturdays and on Sundays for another senior team, into a fat slob. I still feel the damn bad back when the weather is a little unkind, though less so since moving to sunnier climes.

Shortly after my back problems were resolved, and just after the start of the 1956/7 football season—in fact it was in the September of 1956, it was conscription into the armed forces but not before a fairly short term move in employment to the Birmid factory.

This company was about half a mile from home, in the opposite direction from where I had previously worked, but the work was still boring beyond belief, in more ways than one since it involved nothing more than drilling holes in bits of aluminium. No stimulation but more money and, only for a few months before conscription in September 1956. The real downside was no more football with Phillips Cycles, partly because I did not work for them anymore but also because I was unable to train as strenuously as before, and was no longer as fit as I had been. The back problem was still limiting my activities.

The main reason for the switch in workplaces was because my elder sister Edna, who was married to Bill Alford and living in West Bromwich, had a spare bedroom at Roebuck Street in West Bromwich so I escaped cramped Sydenham Road, and went to live with them. Edna is someone who has had a huge influence on my life ever since; still does even though she is now 85. However, more on the influence Edna has had on my life, is for a little later in this tale as I observed earlier.

Edna and Bill later had two sons, Steven and David. Both are now in their 50's, but probably will not thank me for reminding them! Both are married and have grown up children of their own—who in their turn also have children, so, Edna is now a great, grandmother and myself a great uncle!

The older son is Steven who is married to Pamela and their two children are now both grown up, and have children of their own. Steven works for the local council as a litter picker, despite being a qualified glazier. Like his late father, who was also a glazier, Steve decided that the outside winter weather combined with the arduous side of glazing—climbing up ladders and shinning across icy roofs in the middle of winter—should be put aside as he grew older. Steven still works outdoors but minus the risk of falling off a roof! Steve's wife, Pamela, works for the local Sandwell Hospital in the Registry. Their children are Emma and Wayne who are both in their late 20's, and both now have two children of their own.

David is married to Diane, who also works at the Sandwell Hospital, and they have a daughter, Elizabeth. Elizabeth has recently left school and looks forward to a place in higher education. David has had a variety of jobs but mostly in the automobile industry—working both in Birmingham, and also down in Oxford for a time. However, he has recently qualified for the church and is now a vicar.

When Edna's husband, Bill, died a few years ago she was left on her own occupying a three-bed roomed house since both sons were now married and living away from the family home. The old house contained too many memories for her to remain there on her own. She spoke to me of this and mentioned the offer one of her sons had made for her to live with him and his wife. Since Edna and her daughter-in-law were very close, I thought the idea an excellent one. As a result, she decided to go to live in a granny flat which was to be specially built for her on the side of her son's house.

The son who had the granny flat built on to the side of his house was able to do so because his house came complete with attached garage, and bordered on to a large green. The garage was converted and Edna now has her own flat, including lounge, kitchen, bedroom and shower room. When she wishes, she can sit quietly on her own to read or watch her favourite TV programmes or, as is more usual, sit with her son and daughter-in-law. When I say daughter-in-law that is a kind of misnomer as, they are more like mother and daughter. The whole thing has worked out marvellously well for her and her son and daughter in law.

Guess which son she lives with, the litter picker or the vicar? You probably guessed correctly, it is the litter picker.

Conscription and the Royal Air Force

In 1956, and at the age of 18, and in what I seem to recall as being the last full year of conscription into Her Majesty's armed forces, they got me. I applied to join the Royal Air Force and had to complete an intelligence test before entrance, but was accepted. The following year, complete conscription ended and, from then on, the armed forces were comprised entirely of regular volunteers once the last of the conscripted personnel had been demobbed.

Off to Cardington I went, for induction and kitting out over a four-day period. It all seemed fairly friendly and the drill instructors who were there accompanied us on the train to Bridgenorth for basic training—all smiles, card games and affability. I guess it was the money they were making from the card games that helped them to be affable.

Boy, were we wrong about their being friendly! Arriving at Bridgenorth railway station, they turned into a bunch of screaming, pushing, bullying tyrants. Almost thrown on to the back of three-ton trucks along with our kitbags, we hurtled off to training camp. Twelve weeks of marching up and down, gym work, obstacle courses and spit and polish. One element of this early training was that we had to box a one-minute round with someone who was of a similar size and weight. I did not know the first thing about boxing and I lined up with a lad by the name of Cooper. I forget his first name but I should have remembered it because it was an education in not taking people at face value. Cooper, or Coop as he was called by the rest of us, was from the West country of the UK, rather slow of speech and a happy bunny.

Having never boxed myself before this instance, I suggested to Coop that we just go through the motions and pretend. The bell rang, a fist hit me full in the face. He did it again and again, lefts and rights with impunity. By the end of the round I had a bloody nose and split lip, and I had double vision for several days afterwards. What an introduction to the noble art of boxing. However, even cowardly characters like myself try to defend themselves, however incompetently. After about 55 seconds—which felt like two hours—one of the right-hand punches I threw in desperation sailed over his defence and landed flush on his jaw. Coop went down like a log, hit his head on the canvas and was out cold for several minutes. I thought I had killed poor old Cooper and I have never hit anyone since—with one notable and perhaps shameful incident related later—despite suffering extreme provocation on occasion.

A valuable lesson learned for later in life was that when people want to fight because of some dispute, imaginary or real, they have already lost both the argument and the moral high ground as far as I am concerned, or maybe I am rationalising my cowardice. However, the RAF instructors had seen enough of my pathetic boxing skills and despite the knock-out I was never offered the opportunity to box again. I was the most relieved person there.

One result of the first six months in the RAF, and especially of the basic training, was that I grew several inches in height from a little over five foot eight inches to five foot eleven and gained fourteen pounds in weight, but this time it was muscle rather than the fat that followed from my back injury lethargy. I stopped growing at almost six foot tall and around 164 lbs in weight. It has to be admitted the RAF did not serve me too badly in that direction. However, I have let them down since then having now reached somewhere in the region of 200 lbs. I like to pretend the extra pounds are because I have become a well-muscled older person.

After the passing out ceremony at basic training, it was two weeks leave before returning to trade training as an airframe mechanic at Kirkham, located midway between Blackpool and Preston in Lancashire. Close to the Lancashire coast was not the best place to be in the middle of winter. We arrived in late November/ early December, as I recall, where the wind blowing a gale across the Blackpool seafront, when you popped over there, almost had you on your knees.

I had been selected for training as an airframe mechanic and it was at this time that I realised that training and working as a mechanic for five years in the RAF, was accepted as an apprenticeship in Civvy Street. It seemed logical, since I had no other qualifications, so I did it: I signed on for five years and never regretted the decision. I took to the training like a duck to water.

There was real companionship and friendship in the RAF. We trained, and boozed, and laughed and joked, and the weeks flew by until the course was finished and we went off for two weeks embarkation leave before, in our squad's instance, we were to go abroad to become the Levant Canberra Servicing Unit (LCSU), initially to Akrotiri in Cyprus, then to Ta-kali in Malta before returning ten months later to Nicosia in Cyprus.

On the 8ᵗʰ of March 1957, my nineteenth birthday as it happens, we sailed on the troopship Empire Clyde from the port of Liverpool. This was my first experience of leaving the shores of England and it felt rather exotic on a ship weighing over 20,000 tons. That was until the following morning when I went down with sea sickness. Have you ever tried it? If not, do not bother its—horrendous.

The sea sickness was awful until a member of the ship's crew noticing my condition and distress, as I lingered head hanging over the ships rail. He told me to go down to the lowest open deck at the stern of the ship, and to lie down on the benches there for a couple of hours. The crew member's prescribed treatment worked a treat: no sea sickness from that evening and, on the return journey 30 months later I did the same again when we sailed on the sister ship the Empire Orwell back from Cyprus to the UK and, again, no sea sickness. Maybe this is a lesson to be learnt if you are anticipating a sea voyage of your own, though I understand that most modern liners are equipped with stabilisers that keep the ship rock steady when they encounter rough seas, and strong winds.

On the trip out, the Bay of Biscay was allegedly due to be the most turbulent part of the journey but turned out to be almost like a mill pond. Turn left, OK to port if you want to be seafarer technical, and we were in the Mediterranean where it was slightly choppy. However, there were beautiful sunsets of purple and orange, and porpoises (or were they dolphins?) racing in the bow wave of the ship.

Short stops at Gibraltar, Algeria, Malta and Libya to either drop off or pick up fellow servicemen and then it was into Limassol harbour in Cyprus; at least I think it was Limassol though it might have been Larnaca or Famagusta. Time plays strange tricks on the mind.

I guess the one outstanding port visited that sticks in my mind from the trip out was Algiers. There was a wide, natural, sweeping bay spread out in a broad panorama, and dotted amongst the trees, individual houses which were mostly painted in pastel shades of pink, yellow and blue. I imagine that most of the trees that were so much in focus at that time have gone now, due to building developments and the on-set of time.

On arrival in Cyprus, it was a short ride in a three ton truck and we arrived at the Akrotiri airfield. Since Cyprus became independent it has become what is termed a sovereign base, one of several there under which designation NATO has become a factor. To those of you familiar with Akrotiri as it now stands, please remember this was over 55 years ago. At that time, the place was a huge airfield with virtually no accommodation or other facilities. Whoever had the brilliant idea to send us to Akrotiri to service Canberra's must have forgotten that, apart from a few rudimentary services, there was no hanger for us to work in! Also, there was limited accommodation. The Canberra's—B2 bombers and a few photo reconnaissance versions—were there but with nowhere for us to service them!

Ten days after arrival in Cyprus, we were loaded into a Hastings transport aircraft and flown over to Malta, to the Ta-kali airfield in the centre of the island. How exotic can life get for a mere uneducated Black Country lad? First of all travel on a large troopship and now flying for the first time in my life.

By the way, the term Black Country has no racial connotations. It referred to the state of the countryside in an earlier era, around where I was born. This area had many foundries, coal mines, glass-making, and chain- and nail-making factories inside a region surrounded by Dudley, Smethwick, Walsall, and Wolverhampton, which resulted in a blackened landscape during the early part of the industrial revolution. The buildings in the region at that time were coated in soot, and the grass was not its normal green, but black from the deposited soot, hence the 'Black Country' description that has stuck ever since. In calling these enterprises 'factories' this was only partly true for many were also very small manufacturing enterprises, almost like back garden workshops where chains and nails, and such like, were made. These sites also included small glass-blowing sheds where mostly small ornaments were made, such as birds and other animals.

In the centre of Malta, Ta-kali airfield is situated midway between Mdina and Mosta and was to become our base for ten months with the Canberra's being flown backwards and forwards between Cyprus and Malta for their servicing. At least the air crews must have been happy because it gave them a few days' break from flying duties in a more relaxed atmosphere than that which existed in Cyprus, where EOKA were trying to wrest control of the island from the UK and unite the island with Greece. I discuss this in greater detail later in the book.

Like the rest of the lads, I loved Malta but for me it was a contradiction in terms. For us servicemen and women it was almost like being on holiday: work from six or seven in the morning until just one o'clock in the afternoon because of the increasing temperatures. Off to the mess hall for lunch and a kip (sleep!) in the afternoon.

Although not particularly well paid ourselves—I seem to think it was about four pounds per week at that time, with meals and accommodation thrown in, off camp we could eat in decent restaurants in Valetta in the evenings if we so desired. A T-bone steak could be bought that filled your plate, with a side plate of chips, mushrooms, fresh tomatoes, and so on. I seem to recall such a repast cost about two shillings and sixpence in old money. That is twelve and a half pence in new money.

Conversely, a Maltese dock worker earned about £5, I think that was for a month's work though it might have been a week. From that he was expected to pay a proportion to the church, I believe it was expected to be about one tenth of his salary though I may be incorrect in that assumption, it could have been either less or more than that figure; the rest of his income went on paying for accommodation and to feed and clothe a family of maybe six, seven or more. Malta is a highly Catholic country and the churches seemed to be full of gold and silver and rich tapestries. If you are ever in Valetta go to the cathedral—you could go blind from the gold, silver and other valuable accoutrements scattered around.

Another anomaly was the way in which the Catholic priests were treated by the Maltese populace. I have seen pregnant women who were seated at the front of the bus stand to give their seat to young priests. They did not stand for long since my mates and I offered our seats instead. The fact is, it was expected both by the person standing and the priests themselves! I wonder if this is still standard practice? I rather doubt it in a more enlightened age.

For a naïve lad of nineteen, this Malta experience aroused quite a range of diverse impressions. Newly abroad for the first time, new experiences, and wide contradictions in how people lived in different circumstances, in different countries, meant a quite rapid learning curve. Perhaps it was around this time that religion for me became something of a contradiction in terms. For many people, it provides a basis for life and the ways in which life should be carried out. I have no reason to dispute their perceptions, however for me it became something of an irrelevance. I am therefore, something of an agnostic.

Actually, having noted already that I enjoy reading, my current source of enjoyment and information is a book by a lady by the name of Karen Armstrong and, it relates directly to the above paragraph. It's called 'A History of God'. It deals with all religions, including the Christian, Jewish, Muslim and Buddhist faiths.

It tends to reinforce my belief that religion is nothing more than a product of Man's imagination. I stress Man's rather Woman's because it seems to me that, to a greater or lesser extent, religion has been used to legitimise men's control, or should I say perceived superiority, over women. Evidence such as the current argument about the ordination of women and possibly their elevation to bishops perhaps emphasises the control that men still have over the church establishment. For example, I believe that it was a French Bishop, obviously male, many hundreds of years ago, who was given the task of providing an acceptable and authorised first version of the Bible. As such we ended up with only four of the gospels—Mathew, Mark, Luke and John being included.

What happened to the gospels by Enoch, Simon, Judas Escariot and many others? I understand there were somewhere in the region of 35 or more different gospel versions, one was even produced as I understand it by Mary Magdalene and, of course, ignored? By the way why was she subsequently labelled a prostitute? There is little evidence to support it other than early church established doctrine? And there are earlier parallels to this latter attempt to denigrate Mary, see below.

Incidentally, I understand that many of the stories contained within this authorised version of the Bible, particularly in Genesis, have strong parallels with earlier writings from the Epics of Gilgamesh, and other sources from many centuries before. Gilgamesh being a king in Uruk, understood to be modern day Iraq, somewhere between 2,500 and 2,700 years BC. I understand that the stories of the Flood, and Adam and Eve in particular, in the Bible are so similar that they could not have possibly been derived separately from those in the Epics of Gilgamesh. In the Epics of Gilgamesh the story of the flood has Noah as being Utnapishtim. He is informed of the coming flood by the God Ea and Utnapishtim is told to build a boat, the Bibles Ark, despite a coven of Gods being sworn to secrecy regarding the coming flood. The Bibles Flood story is an almost direct copy of the Sumerian story from Mesopotamian antiquity.

Also, in the Epics I believe that in the similar Garden of Eden story, the equivalent people to Adam and Eve were called Enkidu and Shamat. And surprise, surprise, in the Epics, Shamat is a Temple prostitute sent to seduce Enkidu who has been living in isolation after his creation from clay from the river bed. In the bible Adam has been living in isolation in the Garden of Eden after being created from soil, to be joined by Eve, who seduces him into eating forbidden fruit, leading to their downfall. Mary Magdalene, Shamat and Eve, all female, all ladies expressed as exploiting their feminine charms in order to use the male of the species for their own purposes. Who is in charge of church doctrine, the male of the species. What a coincidence!

It is now accepted, that the Sumerians were probably the earliest community to establish other than a hunter/gatherer lifestyle, and to have developed an urban lifestyle. Also, that they were the originators of the first written alphabet and the producers of documents on clay bricks in what is called Cuneiform style. The Epics of Gilgamesh written accounts are alleged to have arisen some 3,700 years ago, but oral tradition is said to have predated this and arisen over 4,100 years ago, preceding the Christian Bible and Judaism by several millennia.

It's also of interest, to note that a different theme for Christianity was put forward by the Gnostics, a group of believers who existed at the same time as Jesus, who presented his ideas in quite a different way to the conventional modern acceptance. I understand that the Gnostics put forward the idea that God existed within each of us rather than as a separate entity outside of us. Doesn't this sound somewhat similar to the idea of Humanism? Is there a parallel? It's also of interest that these Gnostics have, since that period, been labelled as heretics, and excluded from the

Christian church. Maybe I have interpreted all of this incorrectly but it does make you wonder. If anyone out there would like to put me right on my interpretation I am willing to listen, though I doubt it would change my opinion significantly.

As noted above, my liking for 'A History of God' is endorsed by the Sunday Times who described it as *'Brilliantly lucid and splendidly readable. Armstrong has dazzling ability: she can take a long and complex subject and reduce it to its fundamentals, without over-simplifying'.*

The Economist noted *'Only those who think they know it all will fail to be fascinated by Armstrong's search for God'.* While Anthony Burgess in the Observer stated *'Highly readable, and ought to be read'.*

By the way, since some Christians seem to believe that their religion is the first monotheist religion, a religion in which there is only one God, it should be pointed out that, something like 4,000 years ago the Pharaoh Akhenatun formed what has subsequently been acknowledged as the first monotheist God religion, only his God was the Sun. It is an unusual God but at least its tangible and you can see it! Prior to the Christian God, many other God's existed in the human race's perceptions of their world, including

Elohim, El, Baal and Yahweh. For the Greek's there were a whole plethora of god's, including Hermes, Poseidon, Apollo and the chief honcho Zeus; though at least the ancient Greek's included a few goddesses, such as, Athena, Hera and Artemis. For the ancient Dane's too, there were a variety of god's, including Thor and Odin. Going back even further into pre-history, there were the gods of the trees, the rivers, and so on, which were worshipped by the earliest of humans. These were the perceptions of those much earlier folk, concepts arrived at especially by those who wished to maintain some measure of control over others, and wishing to become the elite.

Now some people who have become disenchanted with earthly bound religions look beyond the stars for a superhuman race to come to Earth to save us from ourselves, with sightings of unidentified flying objects, and searches on the planet to find evidence of earlier arrivals, for example, by Erich Von Danikin, *et al,*. One only has to turn on the television these days to find innumerable programmes telling us that ancient aliens have been to Earth in the far distant past, building most of the most famous creations on the planet because clearly, according to them, we could not have produced them ourselves! The Nazca Lines, and most of the ancient cities on the Latin American continent, and of Egypt, are said to have been built using their knowledge and their superior technology! Apparently, according to these advocates, Stonehenge and similar stone circles around the World are also the result of other worldly intervention. For some people, it is even considered that they created us, the human race! Maybe they popped over to the Earth to play around with the genes of earlier species such as the great apes in order to make us who we are.

Whatever happened to the concept of the ingenuity and intelligence of Earth's human race? Have we been so deficient in intelligence in the past that we could not design ways to build Stonehenge, the Pyramids, the Great Wall of China, and the rest? Are we modern humans so arrogant that we cannot believe that the people before us could think, act, and create in much the same way that we do in modern times, given the enormous advantages that modern science has now provided us with? Almost daily, it seems we learn of new things about our predecessors that astound us with their intelligence and abilities. Maybe we have become too blasé and obsessed with our modern science and technology and forgotten those who used more primitive tools in order to express themselves and interpret their world.

Having digressed about religion, or was it a diatribe as some of my friends have described my musings in the past, perhaps a return to my perceptions of Malta is needed. It is not to say I had come from a privileged background myself—quite the contrary, it was a fairly humble working class background— simply, my past was quite different to that I found in Malta. In part it was my time there that made me think more extensively about equality, religion and the expectations that people might have of the life they were expected to lead. My time there made me quite insightful and maybe provided me with an ability to think more laterally about things that I had previously taken as a given. I hope that I still think in a similar way.

Thus, back to some degree of normality and Malta. I managed to get back to the UK for leave that first Christmas in Malta. Flying over to the UK in an RAF transport plane that was almost struck by lightning on the way was an experience in itself. It was a night flight and, as we flew over the Alps gazing down on moonlit snow-covered mountains, you could see tiny lights twinkling in the dark villages giving a profound feeling of isolation that was quite spiritual. Not sure if 'spiritual' is the correct word, given my earlier reservations, but for me personally it was very moving in the relative solitude of that night-time aircraft cabin. I guess it must have touched something inside me but I would claim to be a humanist rather than a religious being.

The flight landed at 12 o'clock, midnight. Believe it or not since it was a Beverley transport aircraft I was flying in, the airfield was Beverley on the East coast of Yorkshire. It was December 23rd and as the cargo doors opened, the iciest gale-force wind blew straight from the sea and into the belly of the aircraft. It almost froze the socks off you. What a contrast to the relative warmth of Malta which we had just left.

The return flight was also auspicious but for a different reason. It was on a British European Airways Elizabethan aircraft. This was a turboprop aircraft that had the first two or three rows of seats nearest the front facing towards the rear, then a small table and the rest of the seats facing forwards. I had an aisle seat facing the rear of the aircraft and seated by the table. On the other side of the aisle, also seated on the aisle but facing forwards, maybe three or four feet away, was a rather overweight elderly gentleman with a balding gingery fringe. He seemed to spend most of the flight dipping a rather large cigar into a glass of what appeared to be either whisky or brandy before putting it into his mouth. At one stage he rose to visit the toilet and, when he returned started looking around for the book he had been reading. His book on Greek mythology was Plato's *Protagoras and Meno*, at least I seem to recall it was that, and he had placed it on my table when he arose. I passed it back to him and he thanked me, or what passed as a thank-you, it was more of a grunt.

When the aircraft made its first stop, which was in Southern France at Nice, a brass band waited on the tarmac together with numerous local dignitaries to welcome the ginger gent. You may have already guessed that I had just travelled seated opposite the legendary Sir Winston Churchill. Even at this later stage of his life, when perhaps his faculties were not as sharp as they had been, he had the most magnetic personality which seemed to fill the aircraft.

Malta was a real revelation in many other ways. For instance, there was what we service personnel called the 'virgins walk'. There was nothing immoral about this perception, though I suppose there are people with different ideas about what is moral or immoral. In the capital, Valletta, the main street was called The Kingsway. I believe that may have changed to something post UK control, something like the Republic maybe? In the early evening you would find, usually two girls together, walking down one side of the street followed by older female relatives a few paces behind. The girls were in their teens and were approaching marriageable age, perhaps 14, 15 or 16 years old. The girls would cross over the street after a few hundred yards and repeat this continually crossing and re-crossing for about half an hour or so. They were, so we were told, on display for potential husbands but carefully monitored by their relatives.

On one particular occasion that I witnessed personally, a girl virtually stopped the traffic. Yes, I know you probably find this difficult to believe because people generally over-emphasise their reminiscences, but it actually happened. Walking with a couple of mates one evening we saw a girl approaching on the opposite pavement. We stopped and stared, in order to get a better look, as the girls strolled down the street. One of them had long jet black hair, a stunning face and figure. The nearest I can conceive would have been a young Gina Lollabrigida, the famous Italian film actress of that era. Who this young woman would eventually marry we would never know but he would have been one lucky man. But, who knows, she may have turned out to be a real tartar. Actually, there is some truth in the perception that if you admire a young woman you should first look at her mother. What the mother is, is what the daughter may become. Am I being sexist? Maybe I am, but I still think that there is an element of truth in the statement.

Running parallel to the Kingsway was a thoroughfare called Straight Street, or more familiarly to service personnel it was known as The Gut. It was mainly comprised of small bars with many of them having entrances similar to those you see in American cowboy films, normally two hinged half-doors. Inside these bars would be three or four small tables and entry would be followed by being joined by one of the girls. Enough said. It was understood by forces personnel that most of Straight Street was owned by the Catholic Church.

As usual, football played a large part in my life, even here in the Middle East. If only some of the overpaid, dilettante, modern day professional footballers felt for the game what people of my era felt, maybe their supporters could relate to them better. At Ta-kali we had the only grass-covered pitch on the island at that time, though to call it grass was a misnomer as it was more like sand paper. You dared not go down in a sliding tackle unless you wanted a skin graft to follow.

Two matches linger in the memory. The first was when our Unit, LCSU, played the RAF military police, nicknamed Snowdrops because of the white cover on their uniform hats. I was playing centre half against a 6 foot 3 inch centre forward of Afro-Caribbean origins. He was built like the proverbial out-house and was very fast. He blew past me two or three times before I decided enough was enough. The next time he tried to skirt past me, I rolled him off my hip. He went up in the air about four foot and was horizontal to the ground. He spun several times in the air, then he hit the grass pitch and rolled. I thought I had hurt him quite badly and ran over to him but he just got up, looked me in the eye and walked away. Needless to say, he had the run of the pitch for the rest of the game. Discretion is the better part of valour, I thought. He was bigger than me and an RAF policeman to boot—no point in pushing the limits too far.

The second game was when the RAF Middle East team played the Maltese champions, Sliema Wanderers, at their stadium. It was a comfortable win by five goals to two for our lads. That was the year that Sliema Wanderers played the English champions, Ipswich Town, and managed by Alf Ramsey, in the European Cup. Although Sliema Wanderers were beaten easily by Ipswich back in East Anglia, Ipswich were unable to get more than a nil-nil draw at Sliema. The RAF team felt quietly chuffed (pleased) about the win and players wondered how they might have got on in the European Cup that year. Oh, the dreams men dream!

Maybe that RAF team success had something to do with the fact we all had long experience of playing on the Maltese pitches. As noted above we at Ta-Kali had the only grass pitch; all the rest were built on the natural kind of sandstone of which Malta itself is mostly composed. These pitches had small hollows and ridges that tended to be invisible to the naked eye after being brushed over before the match. We all knew you could not allow the ball to bounce. In order to make sure you were not to be made a fool of, the ball had to be caught on the chest, or the knee, or the instep of the foot in order to maintain control.

It was while I was in Malta that I almost ended up being charged for making myself unfit for duty. Although I had been over there for about six months and was used to the sun, one day I lay on the beach and dropped off to sleep. That day there had been a hazy sun but not burning hot, however, the following morning when I awoke, my lips were burning and had swollen to about three times their normal size—not quite as bad as that African tribe who wear plates in their lips but moving in that direction.

Off to see the quack down at the medical centre on the orders of Flight Lieutenant Watts who was our Commanding Officer in the Unit. There, the doctor took one look and prescribed a vile pale green ointment that was kept in the fridge at the Medical Centre and, twice a day, I had to visit to have this applied to my lips. I looked and felt ridiculous. Eventually, the skin hardened and I could not open my mouth other than a small gap to eat so everything had to be ingested through a straw. I lived on liquids for several days. Of course, comrades being comrades, this was the perfect opportunity to regale me with the funniest stories they could come up with, some quite filthy.

The result was I laughed, my lips split, and I ended up with blood trickling down my chin. Another version of the old slipping on a banana skin joke—it's funny as long as it is not happening to you!

So what about avoiding the charge of making myself unfit for duty? I was asked by the doctor if I was fit to return to work in the hanger. Unable to speak clearly, I just nodded my head. He smiled and said *"That's good or you would have been spending time down at the guardhouse doing jankers"*. That is RAF-speak for being put on a charge and ending up carrying out menial tasks such as cleaning toilets and picking up rubbish.

Another charming episode in Malta occurred preceding a Battle of Britain display that was to be held at Ta-Kali. We were due to be visited by a number of prominent people and local celebrities for the display. The hard-standing that was used for parking aircraft outside our hanger was to be their seating position. This hard-standing was made of the normal light sandstone prevailing all over Malta and, it was reasoned by some bright spark that it would be too dazzling for these super-stars. The result, we had to paint the whole area green! Talk about cutting the grass with scissors or painting stones around the sergeants' mess white, this beat the lot and it was a large area, big enough for parking two or more Canberra's.

In February of 1958 we were told our sojourn in Malta was to end. Shortly afterwards, we hopped back onto another Hastings and arrived back in Cyprus, this time at Nicosia where they did have hanger space for us to use. Nicosia airfield was well developed, with married families' accommodation

There were also plenty of barrack blocks to accommodate all of the unmarried personnel. However, between these barrack blocks were located what were called 'L-tents'. These were metal framed and constructed from a number of metal sections bolted together with a peaked metal roof and wooden floors. Joe Soap here got one of these L-tents, and I shared it with a Geordie lad from Hexham. We got on OK which was just as well since we were there for twenty months but, though I remember Geordies face, I cannot recall his name.

The working conditions in Cyprus were obviously similar to those in Malta but regarding the weather, it was even hotter. We were up early for breakfast in the mess, then on to the unit's lorry to be driven down to the hanger which was about half a mile or so away, then work from around 6.30am until 1.00pm.

Dress was pretty informal for all of us. The NCOs and officers were similarly laid back and the one thing that could be said for the RAF was that there was little of the formality evident with our army colleagues. For us airmen around the hanger, it was normally to be shirtless and to wear a pair of khaki shorts, and sometimes a beret if we were working outside the hanger, with sandals on our feet most of the time but no socks. Of course, work was usually carried out in the hanger which gave at least some protection from the burning sun, though even in the hanger it was quite hot and humid. Temperatures during the summer could be well in excess of 100f degrees. If you had to work on a Canberra outside, you had to make sure that rubber matting was in place if you climbed onto the aircraft or you could get quite severely burnt.

We had no fridge in which to keep our bottles of soft drinks cold so we improvised and appropriated a steel locker, made it waterproof and laid it on its back. It was an advantage being a servicing unit since we had the creative abilities to change such things to our advantage. When leaving the mess hall in the mornings, we collected plenty of ice and filled the adapted locker. You can't imagine how delicious those soft drinks were when you were gasping in temperatures of over 100 degrees and humidity of 90 per cent plus. Mostly, these drinks were locally produced Orange drinks or Coca Cola, and icy cold. I seem to remember the drinks cost about 10 Mils which was the Cyprus equivalent of just a few pence in old money.

Because of the political situation with EOKA—more of this later—we were confined to camp from Monday to Saturday. On Sundays we were allowed off camp and it was on to a coach and a drive up to Kyrenia on the north coast for lazing on the beach. This was where the officers, RAF and army personnel kept their boats in the local marina. We passed our time picnicking on the beach or buying drinks from a little stall nearby and idling on the sand. Most went swimming—can you believe that I never learnt to swim in those glorious conditions? Still can't even though I now live in the Cyprus of today since my retirement. My efforts now, as then, were merely to go as far as paddling up to my knees in the warm sea.

The most auspicious events on these forays to Kyrenia were when the wives or teenage daughters of one of the married officers or other non-commissioned ranks appeared in their bikinis. Suddenly dozens of pairs of eyes of partner-less, healthy young blokes found something very appealing to focus on. Although there were a few WAAF's on our station they were locked away from us mere airmen, and lived in buildings surrounded by barbed wire owing to being such objects of desire.

The sea was a perfect blue, the beaches covered in fine white sand. I guess that Kyrenia is quite a bit different now but then it was idyllic. Although I have lived in Cyprus for nearly 10 years, I still haven't been back up north to see exactly what it is like. One day I must make the effort to go. Until quite recently, this involved a good deal of bureaucracy about going over to the Turkish held side of the island and it was awkward to go over there and, you were limited about what you could bring back over the border. Fortunately this has eased somewhat so I may make the effort one day when I feel a bit more adventurous. I would also have liked to visit the old Nicosia airfield where I spent twenty months of my service life. However, this is impossible since the airfield now straddles the Green Zone which is the dividing line between the Turkish dominated north of the island and the Greek Cypriot southern areas.

The drawback on these trips up to Kyrenia was that on the coach transporting us to and from the area, we were obliged to have four of our number armed. Two sentries carried rifles and the other two Sten guns, all fully loaded of course. These sentries were to guard us from attack while relaxing during travel and while on the beach—a simple reminder of the situation we were in. Being a sentry was delegated to each of us in turn to share the unwanted duty throughout the Unit.

We were never subject to direct attack though it was never too far from our minds since there were bombings and shootings, though usually it was the army lads who were the target. We did, however have a bomb explode in the NAAFI in RAF Nicosia which killed and injured a number of the lads.

The nearest I got to being killed was by a newly arrived Pilot Officer (PO) who was less than competent in the Nicosia firing pit. All of us lower ranks had to perform guard duties in the various guard towers surrounding the airfield—two hours on and four hours off over a 24 hour tour of duty with a Lee Enfield 303 rifle loaded with ten rounds of ammunition to hand and, a powerful searchlight for company, to scan the areas outside the barbed wire fencing as we looked for potential intruders. Returning to the guard tent at, I think it was either at six or eight o'clock one morning, and having completed a two-hour stint up the tower complete with rifle and searchlight, I walked back to the twelve man tent down a winding path near to where the firing pit was located. Zing, zing, two bullets one to my left, one to the right—whistled past my head. The sound was quite distinct. I froze for a few seconds, then raced over to the pit. There was a Chief Technician in charge and I was still a mere Leading Aircraftsman. However, there are times when rank goes out the window and nearly being shot is a good example. I practically screamed at the Chief *"Some stupid b.....d nearly shot me!"* He knew what had happened but was the soul of discretion. *"It must have been ricochets out of the pit, we must clean the pit"*, he commented, and stopped all further firing. How on earth do you get two bullets ricocheting out of a sand pit in such a manner? Did they both hit the same hard surface in a sand-filled pit and both go in the same direction? With a Sten gun that is almost impossible, they tend to spray bullets everywhere, even over a short distance. I may not be an armourer, but even I know the chances of this happening are almost nil.

The man who I had shouted at did not rebuke me for my language in front of a half dozen young, newly arrived officers because he knew, as I knew, it was the dopey PO at the left of the pit who had pulled the trigger on his Sten gun and jerked the gun to his left, a spray of bullets coming out of the pit and in my direction about twenty or thirty yards away. However, it did occur to me later that, if I had been a few yards either further forward or further back along that winding path, the result might have been quite different. I might have been chewing on a bullet!

On a couple of occasions I have referred to EOKA and the potential for conflict. As with the financial differential I observed in Malta regarding us and the Maltese, this was also a cause for something of a dilemma for me.

Young as I was, the media view, and of course that of most of the UK population, that active members of EOKA were terrorists, did not ring entirely true to me. I assumed that they considered themselves to be fighting for freedom from a colonising power and wanted to unite with their Greek compatriots. Given that little more than ten years previously the UK had been battling to prevent a German victory in Europe, I wondered, even at that time in Cyprus, what would have been the consequences of an earlier German victory? If we in the UK had been occupied by the Germans, would I have had the courage to resist our occupation? If so, would I have been considered a freedom fighter in my country's eyes or a terrorist in the occupying Germans eyes? Probably both, and it was thus with the Greek Cypriots. I guess the devil is in the detail. For me you could not have one view for one country and another for the other. Was there a difference between what the Greek Cypriots were doing and what we might have done had Germany occupied our island? Or what some of the French, Dutch and Greeks had actually been doing during the Second World War? Were they freedom fighters or terrorists? I know what my opinion of this would be.

Perhaps the only thing that gave me pause for thought in all this was that it was not all the Cypriots who were fighting the British presence in Cyprus. The Greek Cypriots in EOKA wanted union with Greece, this was termed 'Enosis'. The Turkish Cypriots, who had lived peacefully with their Greek fellow countrymen for many years did not want the island in a union with Greece since the Turks and the Greeks on the mainland had historically been enemies. (If you would like to get an impression of what life in Cyprus had been before and during the early period of the goal of Enosis rearing its head perhaps a reading of 'Bitter Lemons' by Lawrence Durrell would help. He deals with the situation between 1953 and 1956 when he lived here and prior to the upheaval, though as it escalated Lawrence Durrell rapidly left the island in 1956, a few months prior to my arrival). So it was not all Cypriots wanting the British out to achieve union with Greece. If it had been, I would have thought their goal even more legitimate. Instead, it now became a three-way dispute with some of the more active Greek Cypriots and the British at loggerheads, and the Turkish Cypriots drawn in to a limited extent on the British side since this was in their own interests to do so.

The final result, after several years and within a couple of years after I had left Cyprus, was independence for Cyprus with Greek Cypriot Archbishop Makarios as President and Rauf Denktash, a Turkish Cypriot, as Vice President. The Greek Cypriot majority population, (the ratio seemed to be about 2 to 1 Greek Cypriot to Turkish Cypriot) eventually, again, sought closer links to Greece and a military coup was attempted against the legally elected government of which Makarios was still President. This brought forth a Turkish invasion of the north of the island and a division of this beautiful island that still exists today.

It also begs the question of what would have happened during the Turkish invasion following independence had there not been the sovereign bases established during the independence agreement? Would the Turks have attempted to take on the British forces and/ or NATO forces and complete the takeover of the entire island? Were the British forces obliged to sit in their bases and not interfere? Was there any element of collaboration between Whitehall and the Turkish government? I have heard no hint of a suggestion that this was the case though there may well have been. The Turks had a large standing army and numerical supremacy militarily and, probably could have achieved the goal of occupying the whole island should they have so desired, instead they stopped at the capital Nicosia and just occupied the Northern third of the island.

Did the Greek Cypriots consider then, or do they even now, that maybe the very presence of the British forces on the island that they had sought to remove, and some still want to get removed, perhaps saved them from a complete disaster? One Greek Cypriot writer recently proposed exactly that in the local newspaper.

It must be so easy to have no conscience or to have the ability to consider only one side of an argument or a concept. Unfortunately, or should I say fortunately, I seem to have the capacity to look at all sides of an argument or dispute or situation. Maybe this was one of the reasons why I enjoyed some measure of success as a researcher in later years? There seem to me, to be many people, especially in the political field, for whom the other side of a dispute has no consequence whatsoever. Self interest rules. Perhaps this did indeed give me the insight to become a reasonably objective researcher later in life. At least I do hope so. Maybe it's also in my character to be a bit of a Devil's advocate. I sometimes express views that are diametrically opposite to my own simply to stimulate discussion and maybe raise a little aggravation or debate! Since retiring I think this is the thing—debating—that I miss the most. I suppose I am, by nature, someone who enjoys debate though some say my attempts at debate are boring and tiresome and mere diatribes. Is that my fault or theirs for not understanding where I am coming from? Perhaps some of the ideas covered in this autobiography suffer from this perverse side of my nature.

Returning to more normal things, it was while at Nicosia that I achieved my first paper qualification. I passed the RAF Education Test Part One. This was followed shortly afterwards by passing my technician test to be promoted from a senior aircraftsman to a junior technician. Wow, life was getting high profile at last. (And what have I been saying about self-interest above?)

Because of the constraints on going off-base in Cyprus, we had to find our own entertainment on-base. We did have an open air cinema but you can only sit through the same film a limited number of times and the films did not seem to change too often, or is my memory slipping on this? One period of the day could, however, be guaranteed to bring the camp to a complete standstill. I think it was on a Thursday evening but I may be wrong. At about 8 or 9pm local time, the Goon Show came on the radio and everyone tuned in. If you looked around outside your billet or tent, you would not see a single person on the roads around you and, from every window came the sound of Major Bloodnock, Grytpype-Thyne, Moriarty, Henry Crun, Minnie Bannister, Ned Seagoon, Bluebottle and Eccles—alias Spike Milligan that troubled genius, Harry Secombe the comic and singer, and Peter Sellers, all to become famous worldwide in their Goon and other roles, especially true of course for Peter Sellers who became a major Hollywood star in a number of celebrated films including as the hilarious Inspector Clouseau. The Goons were a required antidote to some of the less amenable aspects of life in Cyprus, their craziness being an antidote to that of our situation with regard to EOKA.

The main attraction on camp, however, was the Friday evening to Sunday night card school. Usually it was Poker, Brag or Chase the Lady. It would start with about eight players and go through the night. As players ended up without any money to continue they dropped out and another player took their place. By late Sunday evening there probably was not a single one of the original starting players left in the game. The amazing thing about these games was that it hardly ever happened that anyone ended up either broke or rich. The money just seemed to circulate, last week's loser becoming next week's winner.

During the winter months the Troodos Mountains in the centre of the island were covered in snow and mist. We only had one opportunity to jump on a coach and visit them during this time of the year and that was only a brief visit as the coach was unable to go far, due to the treacherous nature of the roads on the mountains, barely half way up the mountain we slid to a stop and had to reverse part of the way back down. To compensate, on the way back to camp from this excursion we stopped at a small restaurant for a few beers and a snack and that was our winter outing to the Troodos Mountains over and done with for the duration of our time in Cyprus.

In fact, if we had been able to get there, we could have gone skiing on the mountain and then dropped down to the beach areas and gone sunbathing. Cyprus is normally like that even during the wintertime since from October through to March, perhaps over even longer periods some years, the temperature, even in the winter months, was likely to be around 60 or 70 degrees in the coastal regions. In fact as I write this it is the middle of October and the daytime temperature here in the Paphos region on the south coast is in the high 70s Fahrenheit.

After two and a half years in the Middle-East it was time to return to the UK. Heavier items of personal possessions were loaded into what were called Chitty boxes, wooden chests, to go into the cargo hold of the transport ship. In this case it was the Empire Clyde's sister ship, the Empire Orwell. Off to Limassol/ Larnaca/Famagusta again (still can't remember which it was) and on board ship for return stops at Malta and Gibraltar. We were unable to go ashore at Gibraltar, since it was only a brief stop, but we had a three hour stopover in Malta giving us the opportunity to go ashore, using the small colourful local harbour Dghajsa work boats, and to visit old haunts remembered from twenty months previously.

In my case, it was for a few beers and a meal at one of my old favourite restaurants, remembered from earlier days, before a visit to a local shop that I was familiar with and which I knew sold, amongst other things, high quality watches. We had been unable to do much in the way of off-camp shopping in Cyprus for obvious reasons. It was time to buy myself a little luxury item before returning to the UK. I knew this little shop sold Omega watches, which was what I wanted. I purchased an Omega Seamaster for £21, this was in 1959. I still have the watch on my wrist 54 years later as I write this. It is not merely a little luxury item but a memento of my past and that period of my early life spent in the Mediterranean, and the Royal Air Force.

On arrival in the UK at Southampton, we were ushered into a large warehouse for clearance through customs. We did have certain limits of what we could legitimately import. Mostly this concerned cigarettes and alcohol. No one queried the watch on my wrist. However, one particular army sergeant did feel the full force of the customs officials. On looking through his kitbag and other hand luggage they found excessive cigarettes and alcohol. As a result, they called for his Chitty boxes, already unloaded from an earlier ship, and opened these too. They were full of illegal imports. He was fined a great deal of money and had many of his belongings confiscated.

Now it was off home to await the arrival of my Chitty boxes which contained, amongst other things, gifts for relatives that I had been able to purchase on camp in Nicosia. I seem to recall that we had two weeks' disembarkation leave before having to report back to our new postings in the UK. For most of us who had been in the LCSU it was a posting to number 60 Maintenance Unit (MU) based at Church Fenton midway between York and Leeds in Yorkshire. I stress we were based at Church Fenton simply because we were there only for short periods of time between going out to various airfields in order to repair, or carry out modifications to aircraft.

If it were possible to choose a UK posting in the RAF, then I guess that a maintenance unit would rank quite highly. There were only two such units dealing with aircraft maintenance at that time. The unit we were sent to covered the UK from RAF Gaydon airfield, just south of Birmingham, right up to RAF Leuchars on the east coast of Scotland. The rest of England and Wales was covered by the second unit whose number I do not recall. In the two years with 60 MU, I never had to carry out a single parade or fire picket duty. We travelled in parties of from three or four personnel through to a dozen personnel in three ton lorries all over our area, staying just a few days on some airfields and several weeks on others, depending on the size of the job we were faced with. Because we were only temporarily on these camps, we did not appear on camp lists, and thus were excluded from duties that the permanent camp personnel would be expected to perform.

Since we could be called on to work long hours repairing aircraft, we were issued with cold/wet weather gear: what were termed sea boots and sea boot socks, thick polo neck sweaters, and so on. Some nights we worked through the night to get aircraft ready for a return to flying service. Meals were taken at all times of the day or night, simply because of the pressure on completion of work. As such, we had call on the mess and the duty cook at all times.

One night this led to a little byplay that could have ended with charges being laid against us. At about 10pm on this particular evening, and after a strenuous fourteen-hour day repairing a Hunter aircraft, we entered the mess and asked for our meal. The duty cook offered us what were nothing more than reheated beans, thick greasy sausages that looked as though they had been reheated about five times since breakfast, and thick slices of white bread.

That mess had large fish tanks containing tropical fish, the camp commander's pride and joy so we were told a day later. I am not sure if they enjoyed the bread and sausage they were fed by us though I believe that some, if not all, did survive. The following morning we were called before the Wing Commander in charge of the station to explain our actions. We, of course, told the truth. We had been served with inedible food and had left it on the tables. Someone, perhaps the cook, had performed the dastardly deed and had tried to blame us. We got away with it because there were no witnesses and nothing could be proved against us; and meals from then on were much improved.

On most RAF airfields, just inside the camp gates, an obsolete aircraft would be anchored. This led to another little escapade related to me by another repair squad that could have ended with charges against them. After a somewhat drunken evening, they took a few spanners along and unshackled a Vampire aircraft that had been sited at the entrance to this camp. The fact that the guard house, complete with the MP Snowdrops, was within yards of the aircraft only added to their fun. The following morning the Vampire was found in the middle of the camp parade ground. Yet again, however, although they were the logical suspects they managed to get away with their actions because no one could prove they did it.

This reminds me of another vampire story, only this time it led to my extreme embarrassment. After going home on a 48-hour pass one weekend I arrived back at midnight at an isolated railway station somewhere in Lincolnshire, I forget exactly which camp this was but it may have been Manby. I have to say that this is the first time I have ever related this story to anyone because it was/is so embarrassing. There was no transport from the railway station, so a mile or so walk back to camp was in order on a cold, misty November evening. It was a quiet night with no other people around, and the banks at the side of the lane rose up maybe ten or twelve feet. About half way back to camp I glanced up and saw a figure silhouetted at the top of the bank with mist floating around it. The figure had on what appeared to be a cape spread wide and with the collar turned up. The classic Christopher Lee Count Dracula pose. I froze, and then took off at a run. I suspect that world champion sprinter Usain Bolt would not have caught me over that first few hundred yards. It was only as I entered the camp gates, that I considered that it had probably been some similarly late returning airman who had heard me coming along the lane and decided to have a little fun at my expense with his greatcoat collar pulled up to simulate the Count Dracula pose. The only thing was I had not heard even a hint of a laugh at my expense. Was I lucky, not to have two puncture marks on my neck. Just joking!

It was around this time that a couple of horse racing stories arose that I should perhaps relate. The first involved the same period when my Dracula escapade occurred and we were working in Lincolnshire for an extended period.

The local bookmaker was based in Louth several miles away from the airfield so bets were placed over the telephone and settled when I went over on the Saturday. One Saturday, I had winnings coming back, and the Bookmaker said that something over £11 was due to me. I queried this and said actually it was only a little over £10. He checked his records and came back saying *"If I am a penny short in paying out the customer usually tells me so. No one has ever accused me of over-paying before, and your honesty deserves a reward. Back Granville Greta over the next ten days, but not with me, it will run three times and win three times".* He was slightly out, the second time it ran it finished second, beaten a short head. The other two times it won at 8/1 and 10/1. Maybe having an honest streak in my body paid off on that occasion and, I certainly won a good few pounds from that information.

The second story concerned a local horse trainer located close to our Church Fenton base; I believe it was Les Hall's stable. We became aware of a two year old horse in that stable that was expected to win first time out, but not when it was due to run. For three months I scanned the racing pages looking for this horse. Eventually, it was spotted running at Stockton racecourse—the track has been closed for many years now. The horse, Blue Angel, as I recall, was entered in the last race in a field of about twenty runners. I had five pounds each way since in the morning's newspapers it was not even in the quoted starting prices. When I looked in the following days Sporting Chronicle it had opened up at 16 to 1 and quickly went through every price downwards until starting, and winning at 4 to 5, which was the price I was paid. After three months of waiting for the horse to run I received about £15 for my efforts, a profit of £5!

In all my time in the RAF I never regretted signing on for the five years, except for the last few months. It's strange but, until then, it had felt like a second home to me. As a potential return to civilian life beckoned, I became more unsettled. I was becoming more and more frustrated at having to obey orders and say 'Sir' to little gentlemen who seemed to have only a fancy accent and a junior officer's bar on their shoulder. It's odd how even the thought that I could be promoted from a junior technician role to senior technician, should I agree to sign on for another 3 or 5 years, failed to be all that attractive.

In later years, I did ponder how my life might have turned out had I signed on for a lengthy period. It would certainly have been very different. I certainly would not have experienced the extent of world travel that I have done. I would not have met so many fascinating people. I would not have learnt so much or debated so many interesting ideas across a range of topics, with people from such diverse backgrounds.

Civilian Life Once More

On leaving the RAF, my first two jobs were again associated with the aircraft industry. Why not? This was why I had signed on for five years to get the equivalent of an apprenticeship. However, it proved to be a not very satisfying experience. It seems strange that, having spent five years gaining the qualification for working in the aircraft industry, it quickly became almost irrelevant to my future.

My first job in the aircraft industry in civilian life was with Marshall's of Cambridge. Guess what? Working on Canberra's again. We were converting B2 bombers into PR9s, or was it PR7s? That is, into photo reconnaissance aircraft. Most of the work seemed to be drilling holes in obscure places for the electricians to run miles and miles of cables through to facilitate the installation of the electronic equipment required to carry out surveillance work.

During my time at Marshall's I lived, along with several other personnel, in a Nissen hut on site—not that much different to my time in the RAF as far as living conditions were concerned. This soon lost its glamour, if it ever had any. It was also the case that, in civilian life, the compensating comradeship shared with fellow servicemen and women was no longer there. Instead, it comprised of getting up in the morning, having a quick breakfast then off to the hanger to drill more holes.

There was little in the way of off-work fraternisation since I seemed to have little in common with the workers with whom I shared the accommodation. Much has been said and commented upon, regarding life serving your country in the military but, unless you have experienced it you can have little knowledge of the bonding that takes place. Similarly, the discipline that one is asked to conform to in the armed forces provides social and life skills that are sadly missing amongst many younger people today, who have not experienced the comradeship of military service. It was also so amongst the people with whom I now worked in Cambridge.

Regarding the lack of discipline and social skills thought by many to exist amongst the young, would the reintroduction of National Service be an answer to many of the problems being found amongst younger people in the UK? Many social reformers and civil libertarians would argue against it I assume. What would be their answer to resolving many of the current social problems? To have the freedom to do whatever you desire irrespective of the result of your actions? While I am a great supporter of freedom of action and democracy, surely there are limits that society would find agreeable and acceptable.

Although the pay at Marshall's was reasonable, the environment was not. Unfortunately, the cost of living in Cambridge and away from the factory was too high to justify a move to more amenable accommodation. The environment living on site also ensured that there was little pleasure to be gained from the job and the salary was not great enough to compensate for that fact. I quickly moved on, after just a few months.

This is not to disparage Cambridge itself. It is a beautiful city surrounded by wonderful countryside; at least it was in 1961. I haven't been back since then so it could have changed for the worse in the ensuing years. I guess I have been lucky in the sense that, a few years later, I was to spend two years in Cambridge's equally beautiful, and equally academically acclaimed sister city, of Oxford.

After Cambridge, it was off to the Vickers Armstrong factory, based on the old car-racing circuit of Brooklands down at Weybridge in Surrey. There I worked on the TRS2, a revolutionary new design of aircraft. The TSR stood for Tactical Strike and Reconnaissance. The materials used in the construction of this aircraft were quite different to anything I had worked on before and the nearest type of aircraft to the TSR2 was the American F111, again a swing wing aircraft designed to fly at high speeds and at low altitudes.

Perhaps I should not discuss this aircraft in too great a detail since in order to work on it, I was obliged to sign the Official Secrets Act, under which commitment I believe the implications last for a lifetime. I understand that any discussion of anything that might be considered to be covered by the Official Secrets Act, even in a completely different context, leaves one liable to prosecution, even many years after the actual signing of the Act. However, yet again Vickers Armstrong turned out to be a short-term appointment since in the eyes of the government of the day the aircraft was too expensive to continue to develop, despite the fact it was now in the early stages of flight testing. Instead, they contracted for what those of us working on the TSR2 project considered to be the inferior, though roughly equivalent aircraft, the American F111. After a short period of time I left Vickers Armstrong to return to the Midlands.

I seem to recall that it was at about the same time that the government of the day also cancelled development of the Blue Streak rocket—or was it Black Streak? Whichever colour it was this rocket had the potential to put the UK into the space race which has since proven to be so lucrative that even private commercial companies have entered the field. I believe that many of the British scientists and workers working on the rocket, and on the TSR2, left the UK to go to work in the United States on similar projects. This potential for a commercial space programme now seems to have attracted half the countries in the world intent on getting into space. In addition to the USA and Russia, we now have France, China, India, and even North Korea, entering the field. This also includes a number of private/civilian companies among whom can be counted Richard Branson's Virgin Company. Currently, we in the UK have to rely on the French Arianne rocket or on the Russians to put our satellites into space. Another missed opportunity?

There was one self deprecating event which took place while I was at Vickers which was equally embarrassing as the Vampire story related above. So much so that I am half reluctant to relate it, however, this is my story and the event happened so why not tell it? After all, most of us have been legless through too much alcoholic drink at one time or another. It did lead, however, to my being rather more careful about imbibing too freely, and then driving a motor vehicle, a valuable lesson learnt.

One Saturday morning, we had been working at the Vickers Armstrong site and, together with three colleagues, had decided to go to the Ascot horse race meeting that afternoon. Having had no breakfast before going to work was not a good start. I won a bit and lost a bit on the horses and drank three or four bottles of pale ale at the course, as I recall. Returning towards the bungalow where I was residing, my colleagues decided to stop for a quick drink at a pub very close to the Vickers site. I was hungry but was persuaded to stop for one before returning for a meal at my digs. A major mistake on my part, I started on Bonnie Prince Charlie whisky since I was only intending to have at most a couple of drinks, however conviviality took over and, by the time I left, I had probably consumed nearly the full bottle. To make matters worse, I was still hungry and, at about 9.30pm, I ate a pork pie that I had covered with English mustard. Given that I hate English mustard, this shows how drunk I had become.

Well before 11pm, my other colleagues had left for their digs in New Malden and I climbed into my car to drive the couple of miles to the bungalow where I was staying. Half way there, I encountered a very large traffic island. Approaching the island, I drove up one side of the pavement and down the other. The other side of the island I did the same again. I was very fortunate that the roads were very quiet and free of other traffic and pedestrians. After arriving at the digs the pork pie and I parted company and, once inside the house I woke up at 3am with my arms clutched around the bowl of the toilet. I have to say that this proved a very salutary lesson for me. Suddenly, a little common sense kicked in and I have never driven in such a state again. Yes, I will have a pint of beer or maybe two, and drive, but never more and never when I have felt I have gone over my limit for driving.

The following day (we worked Sundays as well in order to keep up to the schedule on completing the aircraft), all I could do after clocking in was to lie in the back of my car in the factory car park, feeling absolutely wretched and being covered for by my colleagues. For the following five years I could not abide even the smell of whisky. Apart from the seasickness I suffered when going out to Cyprus this was the worst I had ever felt and I cannot honestly recall ever feeling as bad again these many years later. It was a definite lesson in not imbibing too freely, especially to do so, on an empty stomach. However, I have now recovered and I enjoy a tot of whisky now and again. Especially a drop of 18 year old Glenlivet!

After Vickers Armstrong I moved on yet again. This time, as noted above, not into the aircraft industry but back up to the West Midlands and, after a short period of unemployment, to what at that time was the largest engineering employer in the country, Guest, Keen and Nettlefolds (GKN) in Smethwick. At that time GKN employed around 93,000 people most of whom worked in the UK, though there were other factories in India, Canada and some other countries. The wheel had turned full circle for me at that time, back to my origins after about six years away from the area.

The next ten years were spent as a machine tool-setter making screws of varying types and sizes. Fortunately, GKN had an in-house training section and I quickly learnt the basics of running what were termed heading machines. All this machine did was feed large coils of wire of different dimensions into various die forms to form the head of the screw. After a short while I became the leading hand with a group of four other setters working with me. Strangely enough, in many ways this was a more satisfying job than that in the aircraft industry. Each day seemed to hold different challenges and problems to resolve and I enjoyed the responsibility of running the section.

Perhaps the one drawback was that the company operated a two shift per day system. One week we would be working from 6am until 2pm and the next from 2pm until 10pm. However, it's amazing how the body can adapt to such changes in the sense that one week, on the early shift, I would only get five hours sleep from midnight until about 5am. The following week maybe eight or nine hours sleep from midnight until 8am or 9am.

As the leading hand it was my job to manage the group of about 30 machines, and make sure we achieved the maximum bonus each week. Anything over the maximum and we lost that part of the bonus completely, anything below, and we had failed to get the best return for our week's work. In order to make sure that we were spot on with the bonus, I purchased a calculator from the local Boot's the Chemist store. It was one of those early versions which could be recharged, now they give such calculators away with a couple of gallons of petrol. At that time, in the mid 1960s calculators were extremely expensive and this one cost about £40, a fair expense at a time when my wages were less than £20 a week. However, it was worth it because, week after week, we maximised our bonus and never logged in any excess.

I was very conscientious and always made sure my machines were operating well, taking longer perhaps than many other setters in setting them up. As a consequence they seemed to run longer and more efficiently. Strangely enough, this also meant that I spent far less time on maintaining my machines, or repairing breakdowns, than any of the other setters. One day the mill manager walked past as I was reading a newspaper and drinking a cup of tea. He made some remark about my not being paid to read newspapers. I took him around my set of machines and noted that all were running, and producing good products. I mentioned the fact that I was paid to produce products for sale and, make a profit for the company and, that my reading a newspaper indicated I was doing exactly that. He smiled and walked away. He did not bother to comment again if he ever saw me reading or imbibing a cup of tea.

GKN at that time was a very paternalistic company and many of my work colleagues' families had worked for the company for generations. Two brothers, a little older than me, had over thirty years service between them by the time I left the company. Their father and two uncles had each worked for the company for over forty years.

While there were many friends at GKN, occasionally someone would come out with a surprising approach. One Friday evening, shortly before I left GKN and as we were clocking out at 10pm, the person behind me, who I had hardly ever spoken to other than saying hello, came out with a surprising comment: *"You enjoy a bet now and again don't you"*, he remarked. That was a bit like asking the Pope if he was Catholic. Of course I enjoyed a bet. I had spent half my life backing horses. I only knew the man who addressed me as Paddy, though I knew he had been warned off virtually every dog track in the UK for being involved in dubious betting activities. *"There is a dog running tomorrow"* he said *"You can put your mortgage money on it"*. Actually I did not have a mortgage but I understood what he meant. The greyhound was running at what at that time was called a 'flapping track'. This meant it was not part of the Greyhound Racing Association approved tracks, and where apparently some rather dodgy dog racing could take place.

As I have mentioned earlier, I am not a fan of greyhound racing but, at that time, I had won a reasonable amount of money from the bookmakers backing horses so, although I was not particularly into greyhound racing, this seemed to be too auspicious to ignore coming from this chap. The following day

I visited four different bookmakers and at each one I placed a £50 bet to win on this dog. The dog was running in the last race at the meeting and was racing against the track champion which had never been beaten out of the starting traps. The traps opened and the dog that I had been tipped flew out ahead of the track champion. It led at every bend and romped home at 3 to 1. I had won an enormous £600, plus my £200 stake money back. There was one slight drawback to the result. I had also placed a £40 forecast on the track champion coming second to my selection and it got beaten by a nose virtually on the finishing line to finish third.

This was over 40 years ago and heaven knows what that amount of money would equate to these days. Needless to say Paddy had a nice little bonus from me, though he never did gave me another tip. I still remember the dogs' name, the lovely Jane Penny. The dog ran twice more at the track and I backed it each time and it won each time, though now it was at a much shorter price, in fact odds on. I never saw any mention of the dog ever again, either at local tracks, or around the country. It was as though it had disappeared. Either that or its name had been changed as it toured around the less regulated dog tracks.

After several years at GKN there occurred an incident that brought home to me how tenuous long term service was and raised an element of uncertainty in my mind about GKN being my ultimate goal for another thirty-odd years of service. It occurred one bitterly cold December morning when we were working the early shift. As usual, I arrived at about 5.45am and, shortly afterwards, one of my setters—we called him Little Sid—sorry I have forgotten his surname, arrived. He lived about a mile away from the factory and, as usual, had walked to work. He was as white as a sheet but still sweating. It was clear he was ill. With some difficulty, I made him sit down and sent another of the lads across to the on-site surgery for the duty nursing sister. She arrived with a wheelchair and we moved him over to the surgery. I explained to the sister that he had complained of pains in his left arm and had a history of chest problems. The danger signals were clear and I suggested that she should send for the duty doctor immediately or call for an ambulance.

Just after 8am, I went over to the surgery to see how things had developed. I was appalled to discover Sid had said he just had a cold and she had believed him. The sister had ignored my advice, and her own alleged medical expertise, and had put him in a back room to lie down. I made it clear that unless a doctor was called immediately, there would be repercussions. Even with my minimal understanding of medical matters I believed he had had a heart attack, that it might have been only a mild one, but a warning he was quite ill. When I checked an hour later, I discovered that, when the doctor arrived, Sid was dead. He had lain in that back room on his own and passed away. Poor return on his commitment to GKN, though this had not been the company's fault but that of the nursing sister for ignoring her own training. Who is to say that he might still be alive today if he had received prompt medical care, though he would now be over a hundred years old?

Little Sid had worked for GKN for six months short of fifty years and was shortly due for retirement. He had a perfect attendance record, something he was so proud of he had walked to his death to maintain it. If anything was designed to bring home to me that loyalty at work was not the be all and end all of life that was it. However, I am a bit of a hypocrite regarding so-called loyalty since, a little later in this diatribe; I harangue modern-day representatives of the football world for their lack of loyalty to their supporters, but more of that later.

Shortly after this episode with Sid, I became the shop steward for the heading mill where I worked. I represented the Amalgamated Union of Engineering

Workers (AUEW). Little did I know at that time that this was to be part of a development that was to change my whole life? At that time, while I was a shop steward at GKN, the AUEW convenor was a chap by the name of Bill Jordan. He was eventually to become the President of the Union and finally General Secretary of the International Confederation of Free Trade Unions. Bill became Lord Jordan and finally in the year 2000, Baron Jordan of Bourneville and a Commander of the British Empire (CBE). I understood that, as a Labour member of the House of Lords, he was still active in politics.

It was shortly after originally writing this last couple of paragraphs that, curiosity aroused, I decided to contact Bill once more to see how his life had progressed from his own personal standpoint. I forwarded an email to Bill via the House of Lords since I had no other means of contacting him. A couple of weeks passed with no reply so I guessed that maybe he was away on holiday. Then, one evening, the telephone rang in my little apartment here in Kissonerga and my old colleague, who I had had not seen or contacted for about forty years, was on the line. What a joy. We spent about 40 minutes reminiscing about the old times and people we knew and the things we had done. I cannot recall a more pleasant conversation since I retired those many years ago.

He had not responded to my email because he was no fan of the technical changes, such as emails and telephone texts, that have occurred over the years, and which I had become so converted to. Maybe his reluctance to use such devices, and my continual use of them was a consequence of my work on new technologies, explained later in this story, while Bill was much more a person-to-person man for whom the social context of interaction was what mattered. I guess, in a sense, this was the exact opposite to that view of life extolled by Margaret Thatcher, for whom social interaction seemed unimportant to the extent that only the self seemed to be important—or at least that was the impression gained—to the detriment of social society.

On reflection, it may seem odd or strange, or maybe just a coincidence that two shop floor workers from GKN, such as Bill and myself, should have taken such paths in our later lives. Bill was an engineer by trade and myself an aircraft fitter by trade and a machine tool setter by inclination, yet neither of us ended up working in factories, and both ended up in a sense carrying out occupations a considerable distance from work on the shop floor.

During our telephone conversation I recalled something Bill had said 40 years before on discovering that I had earned a place at Ruskin College. He noted at that time that there were two approaches to learning. The School of Life, and the School of Academia. Bill had taken the School of Life approach and I, after a period of the School of Life, rather late in life had taken the other approach. Bill through hard work and political astuteness had led two major trade union organisations, and earned a seat in the House of Lords after leaving GKN. I myself had worked for a number of highly regarded national and international organisations and travelled widely carrying out research, attempting to spread the word about the technical and organisational changes I saw taking place. However, I seem to be getting ahead of myself regarding changes in my own life and relating developments in my own career which are best left to the appropriate place later in this little story.

To return to my shop steward life, I guess I have always tended to believe that, if you do a job of any kind, you should do it the best you can. Is that a tautology? As a result, on becoming a shop steward for the AUEW I signed up for a union organised correspondence course. It was called 'How to be a Shop Steward' now that is a novel title for a shop stewards course I guess! The course was run by the Trades Union Congress (TUC) from Scotland, I think it was at a place called Kirkentiloch, but it might have been run from the moon for all it contributed to my knowledge and skills. Each time my answers to a set of questions posed by them, and to which I had replied, was returned to me they only contained a tick or a question mark, or a 'How' or a 'Why' against a particular sentence or paragraph. The feedback was appalling. How the hell was anyone expected to learn anything without coherent feedback?

Never one to give up too easily, I completed the course to someone's satisfaction but not my own. However, I then applied for a Social Sciences course with the TUC and that is where I really struck lucky. Do you recall my comments earlier about good luck/good fortune? This course was one of the first that the TUC had carried out on an experimental basis with the National Extension College (NEC) in Cambridge, which had been established ten years before in 1963. I believe up to 300 union members became students with the NEC at that time (not sure if that has continued), after being recruited for NEC courses.

The second massively lucky break was the tutor I was allocated. This was a man I never met or even talked to personally, but who probably led to my career-changing life. His name was Sam Rouse and I believe he had been a head teacher, and that he had lived in Cumbria for much of his working life. Each essay I sent to Sam came back with detailed comments and suggestions for further reading, not always related directly to the course. I think I must have become a bit of a pest at the West Bromwich main library, requesting somewhat specialist books that they had to keep calling for from other libraries because they did not have them on their own shelves.

The completion of this course was diametrically different to the first one. It changed my whole perception into wanting to learn even more, and of where I wanted to go now, and another lucky break provided the answer. Reading the AUEW monthly magazine I noticed that, on the inside back page there was an advertisement for another learning opportunity. It was for admission to Ruskin College in Oxford. It called for a 1,000 word essay on one of six nominated topics and, if invited then to go for an interview at the College. This Ruskin approach seemed a step too far since I had no academic qualifications other than my auspicious RAF Education Part One! The thought of even attempting to qualify for Ruskin was not merely daunting but rather frightening.

Ruskin College is something of an anomaly in Oxford since it was designed purely for mature students who had perhaps missed out on education first time around. It was also primarily for people who were involved in the trade union movement. It was in Oxford but not formally part of the University system, though some of the Ruskin students did take University courses and we would have access to some of their seminars if we wished, also access to pretty well all the libraries in Oxford. I wrote to Sam and explained what I was considering and the fact I had considerable doubts about trying for Ruskin. I also gave him the title of the essay that I was thinking about trying if I did attempt it. He could not have been more enthusiastic in his return two-page letter and told me I must try. Included with the letter was a list of books I should read if I did tackle that topic. The library was going to have to be busy again!

The topic I had chosen to respond to, and which was one of six options Ruskin College posed in the advertisement was, 'Is civil disobedience ever permissible in a democratic society? At least I think it was expressed as 'permissible' I may be wrong it was a long time ago, but I am almost sure that was the word used. I decided to give it a go and I read extensively and used three examples from ancient and modern history to argue it was 'permissible'. The first was the example of Martin Luther King and his civil rights campaign in America which was then current. As a second case study, I used the example of Mahatma Gandhi and his non-violent campaign over many decades in India against British rule, and his subsequent imprisonment. Finally I posited the example of Socrates and his fate for defying his peers in the education of youth in what is now recognised as the world's first democratic society. On reflection, it is strange to think that all three of these examples were of men who died quite violent deaths for their beliefs. Two by assassination and the other through enforced suicide by drinking a poison called 'Conium' which was derived from an umbelliferous plant almost certainly identified as hemlock maculatum.

The idea of actually having to write 1,000 words in support of my ideas was daunting at the beginning. The longest piece of writing I had done previously was about a hundred or so words for the shop stewards course in response to a specific question, apart from the odd one-page letter home while in the Middle East and I had seldom been much of a letter writer. I am still the same now, and a quick email or text is my modern answer to an exchange of messages. However, after about six or seven weeks of reading and sweating over the essay, it was submitted with considerable trepidation. Since I had no typewriter or computer, the essay was produced in longhand, and my handwriting is not the greatest thing to behold. I am not sure whether it was relief or unmitigated terror when several weeks later a letter arrived inviting me for interview.

I arrived in Oxford, with all that that city entailed about education, and eventually arrived at the college in Walton Street. The walk from the railway station past various colleges was knee trembling in itself. In fact, at that time Ruskin College was just over the wall from Worcester College in Walton Street (Ruskin College has since moved to Old Headington just outside Oxford itself), and I entered, spoke briefly to someone in the reception area and was ushered into a waiting room. Shortly afterwards I was directed into a small office.

The interview itself only took about half an hour and only one lecturer was present. I am afraid I have forgotten his name, though I can clearly remember his face. At one stage the interviewer left the room and I noticed my essay on his desk. Written on the bottom were just three words. 'Interesting and thoughtful' I was not sure whether that was positive or negative, given, that only three words were appended.

Two weeks later, I received a letter inviting me to attend Ruskin College on a Social Sciences course for a period of three ten week terms per year over a two year period. I was stunned. What the hell had I got myself into? I had left school with no qualifications and, apart from my RAF Education Part One bit of paper, was really totally uneducated academically.

Fortunately, my five years in the RAF and my service abroad had provided some measure of self confidence and, had made me think a bit differently than might have been the case otherwise. My group leadership and shop steward role at GKN had also helped and, without those experiences, I might not have accepted the offer but I did and the next step was to discuss it with my employers.

As an aside, while at GKN I had noticed an advertisement posted by MENSA for a qualifying examination at Aston University. I decided—not too sure whether it was curiosity or arrogance—but I quietly contacted them without telling anyone else and arranged to attend. I sat a two or three-hour test; not sure which now as it happens, but I think it was three hours. This was along with many other similarly curious people and I awaited the result. Two weeks later a little slip of paper arrived in a small envelope, the enclosed note was a strip of paper about four inches by six inches and noted that the score I had achieved indicated an IQ of 143. They remarked that this equated to a level of the top 3 per cent of the UK population since the average I.Q was 100. However, I should point out that, given that millions of brain cells have died since that period of time, I no longer lay claim to being particularly bright.

Having received the offer from Ruskin College, I approached the management at GKN with the hope that they might give me leave of absence for thirty weeks a year for the next two years! Some hope, I thought. Despite thinking it would be unlikely they would agree I had built up quite a good reputation, both with my workmates and the management, over the previous nine years both through my work for the company and my union activities and, somewhat to my surprise, the company agreed to my request. I think, in part their agreement was because, in many ways GKN at that time, and through many previous decades, had been a very paternalistic company—as I noted earlier—and dealt with its employees in a very open handed way not typical of many other employers in the UK at that time. In fact, my shop steward's work had at times seemed more like social work than being of any confrontational nature, as much working with the management in resolving shop floor problems than against it and that worked in my favour. Often, we cooperated in helping individual workers rather than clashing heads. In fact, there had not been a strike at GKN in the Heath Street, Smethwick plant since the 1930's. However, this was at a time when the papers were full of the car workers' clashes led by a man named Robinson, and whom the newspaper media liked to call 'Red Robbo' A union convenor in a Coventry car plant who was being portrayed in some parts of the media as the stereotypical trade unionist!

As an example of how this collaboration worked out at GKN, one particular instance of my union activities at GKN stands out. One of the lads had got into financial problems and he, and his wife and children, faced being evicted from their home. I approached the mill manager and discussed the problem with him. We came up with a support package, provided by the management, which allowed him to pay off his debts and repay the company over a period of time. In this way he kept his home, the management retained a good worker, and the union came out with an enhanced reputation.

Another incident that I recall, involved a labourer of Afro-Caribbean descent who was to be sacked for fighting. He was a member of our union, though not a very popular character with our members on the shop floor owing to his being quite rude and aggressive. However, I decided to find out exactly what had taken place and interviewed both parties to the incident. It turned out there had been no fight, the other person involved admitted he had merely been pushed in the chest and confessed that he had racially abused the other man. I went back to the manager and stated that, yes, we agreed there had been some measure of assault and the man could be sacked but that the other man—belonging to a different union—must also be sacked for racially abusing him. A little bit of psychology being tried on my part and this gave the manager pause for thought given this could involve complications between the two unions. He agreed the man could stay, but not in our mill and provided I could find alternative employment for him. The responsibility for his employment had become mine!

I approached the foreman in the tool room, one of the most important departments in the company, and he agreed to take the man on for a month-long trial. One month later, I entered the tool room to be greeted by our member with a big grin on his face and was given a high five. The foreman said he was one of the hardest working workers in the shop, would do any job he was assigned, and was very popular with everyone. My original assessment of him was that his moodiness while working as a labourer in our shop was down to feeling bad about his job, and his low self-esteem. His girl-friend was a nursing sister at the local hospital and, he a mere labourer, moving pans of work around the shop. Now, with a more responsible job and feeling valued by the new managers and his new workmates, he had responded in the way I had hoped he would.

After digressing about my shop stewards role, perhaps it's time to get back to the Ruskin versus employment issue. I was to be allowed to return to the company for the vacations and this would enable me to maintain some measure of financial stability, since the student grant was less than half of my then wage with GKN. This was at a time when students in higher education were offered some small measure of financial support, unlike now when students incur huge debts that require half a working lifetime to repay, if they ever are repaid.

However, before leaving this part of my life story, I would like to note that, while at GKN on a full-time basis I had reason to dispute the commonly held belief, which seemed to be encouraged by the newspaper media, that British workers were resistant to technical change because it would lead to job losses. At GKN, our workers welcomed new technologies. In part this theory of opposition to change has a long history, harking back to what were termed the Luddites. These were men, or mostly men, who broke up machinery at the time of a major change from the cottage industry base of the textiles industry to factory-based production using new machinery.

I cannot believe that GKN were alone in being able to introduce faster machinery into their production systems since the personnel there were most willing to introduce new systems in our mill. The reason is quite simple and could be called self-serving. Those who managed to work on the new machines were more likely to earn more money and, similarly, were more secure in their employment. Maybe employers should start to think more positively about new technology and, how they strive to introduce it. I have always found that consensus is far more profitable to both the employer and the employee than confrontation! Look at the example of the Germans, the Japanese and the Swedish employers/employees who work on the basis of consensus rather than conflict.

Myself as a gauche 15 year old with sister Edna, 1953.

Colleagues at Phillips cycles, on lunchtime
canal bank break, 1954.

Troop ship Empire Clyde en route to Cyprus, 1957.

Valetta street scene, Malta, 1957.

Palace in Valetta, Malta, 1957.

Some of the LCSU lads having fun, Ta-Kali, Malta, 1957.

Levant Canberra Servicing Unit group photograph
with Canberra aircraft, Nicosia, Cyprus, 1958.

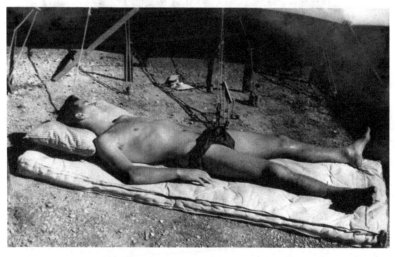

Sneaky photograph of me between tents
sunbathing, Nicosia, 1958.

LCSU Xmas party in billet Pub! Nicosia, 1958.

LCSU Xmas party entertaining NCO's, Nicosia, 1958.

NCO's imbibing at Xmas party, Nicosia, 1958.

Group of students and staff, intake of 1974,
Ruskin College, Oxford.

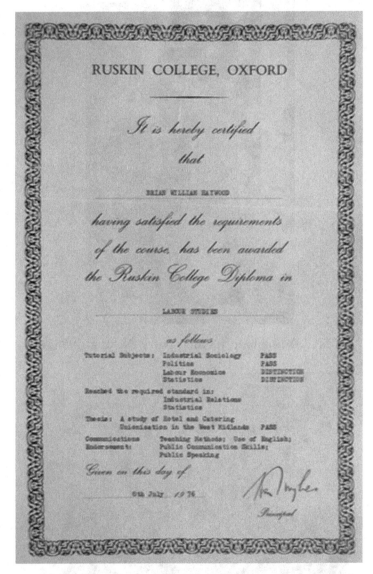

My first academic qualification, Ruskin Diploma, 1976.

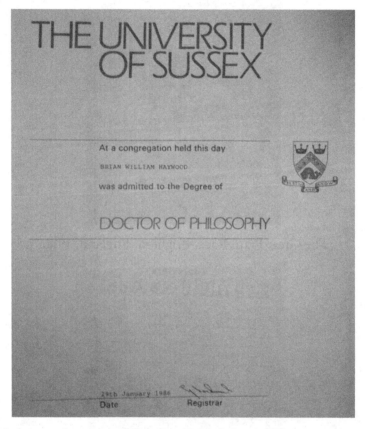

THE UNIVERSITY
OF SUSSEX

At a congregation held this day

BRIAN WILLIAM HAYWOOD

was admitted to the Degree of

DOCTOR OF PHILOSOPHY

29th January 1986

Date   Registrar

My last academic qualification, D.Phil, Sussex University, 1985.

The Great Pram Race, Brighton, England, 1986.

BET	No. of Selection	Singles	Dbles	Trbls	4 Folds	5 Folds	6 Folds	7 Folds	Total Bets
Patent	3	3	3						7
Yankee	4		6	4	1				11
Canadian	5		10	10	5	1			26
Heinz	6		15	20	15	6	1		57
Super Heinz	7		21	35	35	21	7	1	120

Selections — Meeting/Time

1	CLARENTIA	3·05 N
2	VERD-ANTIQUE	4·10 N
3	GOLD FEE	4·40 N
4		
5		
6		
7		

7 Bets at £10 'per unit = Amount Staked 70·00

Tax – see Fair Play Rules poster for definition.   Tax 7·00

Please keep this copy, it is your receipt. All bets accepted subject to rules.   Total Stake 77·00

Ladbrokes betting slip, my big win leading to the Arc visit, 1986.

Family group, sister Edna, nephew Steven,
David's wife Diana, nephew David, Edna's husband Bill
and Stevens wife Pamela, 1987.

View from Central Park, New York, USA, 1988.

Beach scene near Rio de Janeiro, Brazil, 1988.

Midnight on lake near Ivalo, Finland, 1988.

Another mid-summer midnight photograph
on Lake at Ivalo, 1988.

Ex-Empress Maria Theresia's Summer Palace,
Laxenburg, Austria. Site of IIASA, 1990.

Park view of back of Summer Palace, Laxenburg, 1990.

Island castle in park lake behind Summer Palace, 1990.

Another view of the Palace park, 1990.

Sunlit square in Warsaw, Poland, 1990.

The Coliseum in Rome, Italy, 1991.

The Trevi Fountains, Rome, 1991.

Scenic view in Rome, 1991.

Concert site in old quarry in St Polten, Austria, 1991.

Another shot of converted quarry, St Polten, 1991.

American Big Al and myself in hotel bar in Paris, France,
at United Nations darts tournament, 1991.

IIASA Conference reception at Gumpoldskirchen,
Austria ,1991.

Conference dinner, Gumpoldskirchen, 1991.

Photograph of IIASA conference participants
at IIASA, Laxenburg, 1991

Another view of participants, Laxenburg, 1991.

Myself chairing the IIASA conference, Laxenburg, 1991.

John Young, Bob Hallett and myself celebrating Nigel
Mansell's winning of the F1 championship, 1991.

Two of the ladies charming the guests at a United Nations barbeque at John Young's home in Vienna, 1991.

The old town square in Prague, Czechoslovakia, 1991.

The famous Karlov Bridge in Prague, 1991.

Captain of Sicasa darts team winning Manchester
Cup with Rita, Heiki and Jari, Vienna, 1991.

Social evening in Vienna with UN colleagues, 1991.

Beach scene at Flic en Flac, Mauritius, 1991.

Group of participants at Brighton UN darts tournament, 1994.

Two old wrecks in Lanzarote, 1994.

The famous Lakeside, England, darts venue
with another UN get together, 1994.

Another photograph from Lakeside, 1994.

View of Amsterdam, Holland while at a conference there, 1995.

Imbibing while seeking a home in Cyprus, 2003.

Paphos Harbour, Cyprus, 2005.

Civic reception for West Bromwich Albion following
promotion to the Premiership, 2007.

Fan's celebrating Albion's promotion, 2007.

Myself looking somewhat thoughtful!, 2007.

My Kissonerga, Cyprus, home complete with sunbed, 2008.

Why I live in Cyprus, sunshine with a cold beer
and a newspaper to hand!!!.2012.

Further and Higher Education

At the beginning of October 1974, I arrived one Saturday afternoon, suitcase in hand, at Oxford's main line station to be greeted by a group of what were now second year students with a transit van. As I recall there were two other new students arriving at the same time as myself. I don't think any of us new arrivals had much of a concept of what we were letting ourselves in for.

We were driven, not to Walton Street in Oxford but to what were the first year students' residences at what had previously been a large private house and at one time a residential school in Old Headington, a suburb just outside Oxford itself. I found myself allocated a room in a wonderful old four-bed-roomed cottage, about fifty yards from the main house that was now the main Ruskin first year students' building, containing a refectory, teaching rooms and a top floor of bedroom accommodation. In addition to this building and my particular cottage, there were two other residential buildings, one was of a more modern design, and one a converted stable block.

By Sunday afternoon, all the new students had arrived. I believe there where 60 of us in the intake and from all sorts of UK regions and backgrounds, including a number of African students who were financed by bursaries. It needs to be stressed that Ruskin at that time was primarily for people of a trade union background, normally shop stewards, probably still is. I stress primarily because there were a substantial number of students with a social services background training to be social workers, though they were also members of their own trade unions. However, we all linked in well together in what became an intensely stimulating environment.

Returning to Ruskin for the first time for over 30 years last summer I was struck by the feeling that the place had changed somewhat, or was it myself that had changed? It just felt different. Of course it was vacation time and, only a few students had remained during the vacation and the people I knew and had debated with were no longer there. When I visited and spoke to the students and members of the staff it seemed not to be the cauldron of the 1970's but how could it have been without those people with whom I had shared those times? And I had certainly changed over the ensuing years, so I guess my impressions were tainted by those changes in myself as well. As I noted, I only met members of the staff and several students who were spending the summer in the residencies but the feeling of difference persisted. Was it more establishment oriented, or just my nostalgia for the past? Maybe if I had visited during term time my impressions would have been quite different.

Looking around at our first formal introductory meeting on the Monday after my original arrival at Ruskin I was struck by one thing in particular; the age of my new colleagues. As noted above the College was founded to cater for a second chance in education for people who had missed out first time around and the norm was, I believe, to be at least 23 or 24 years old through to the 30s. The majority in my year were mid- to late 20s and a few in their early 30s. It quickly became apparent that I was the daddy of them all at 36 years of age!

That first evening at Headington, and on entering the main entrance hall, I noticed that a blackboard had been placed on top of a radiator with the chalked message, 'CP meeting room 62, at 8pm tonight' Maybe I was a naïve 36-year-old at that time but I did not have a clue what the C.P initials stood for. I learned at the first full meeting of the first year student body that it was the Communist Party and that, in the following elections, all three positions of President, Secretary and Treasurer for our year were won by members of the Party, and the meeting had apparently been to organise this. I understand there were only about half a dozen or so CP members in my intake but they were clearly well organised.

Now, I am not for or against the CP or against being organised, since I was and still am a liberal but committed trade unionist, but I do like to see fair play and have never been keen on backroom control by any group, either of the right, e.g. the public school Bullingdon Boys who are now so prominent in the Conservative Party, Parliament, and the Cabinet; or of the left, the CP or similar groups. As a result, at the beginning of the second year I played a little game of manipulation myself, perhaps just to see if it could be done and as an exercise in organisation. It actually worked. I went to one of my colleagues, who I will call Richard, and suggested he should stand for President and that I and several others would support him. Of course, there were no others, it was just me. Having established a student President candidate, I then approached a second friend, whom I will call Colin, and suggested he should stand as Secretary and that Richard, I and others would support his nomination. Finally, I approached a third friend by the name of Dick (he preferred this to being called Richard unlike Richard), and repeated my ploy. With four of us in the plot, I suggested that each of us approach people who we thought would support our slate of candidates, which we all did.

All three were successfully elected as student representatives: President, Secretary and Treasurer! It was not all that difficult since it was all down to a bit of sleight of hand on my part. By the way, I never wanted any part of being a representative at Ruskin myself. It was just an exercise to see what could be achieved and maybe to make sure no political party had control of decisions that should have been more properly democratically based, though I suppose what I did could be considered anti-democratic in itself.

At this point, I cannot continue without a digression about the traditions of Oxford University. For example, in order to use the Bodleian Library we, as a new intake at Ruskin, had to register in a formal ceremony at the library. We lined up together with several hundred other new Oxford students of that year, most of whom were in their teens, and we were led into a large hall at one end of which was a long table behind which sat several people. The queue wound around the walls of the room. On reaching the table, one at a time, we each had to hold a declaration in our hands and swear not to burn down the Library. This, of course, dates back to the time when the Library was lit centuries before by candles for reading purposes, but it does highlight the traditions that remained firmly in place at that time.

Do they still do this at the Bodleian? I guess they must since it has been going on since time immemorial. Personally I found this quite humiliating and resented the whole process maybe that was down to my feelings of inferiority? Actually, I never ever used the Bodleian as a result of this experience preferring the smaller less formal libraries dotted around Oxford, particularly the library that focused primarily on statistical analysis. However, I have been informed recently that it appears that the more mature Ruskin students' enjoy the Bodleian experience. I have to say that for myself still, to this day, I feel the whole ethos of this Bodleian experience highlights to me the differences that exist between the haves and the have-nots in our society. Is this ceremony just a formal exercise based on historical precedent or a bid to make sure everyone knows their place in society; despite the fact that I have been made aware that actually it is considered a security measure aimed at preventing basic theft and damage, and that apparently it works.

Despite all that followed over almost the next 30 years, university, secondment abroad, international travel, conferences, presentations, publications, Ruskin remains the most challenging and stimulating experience of my life. I think of the place and the people I shared the experience with a great deal, and with much affection. Ruskin seemed to provoke ideas and concepts in me that were completely new; the people, fellow students perhaps as much as or even more than our tutors, passing on their experiences and ideas, a type of reading matter that was completely new to me. It was a real melting pot. We even had our own bar in the basement where discussions could turn very heated, though never violent. At one point, the bar was closed down as being too disruptive and, for keeping students up into the early hours—it had no closing time and was staffed by the Ruskin students themselves.

The Ruskin bar was also popular with some of the students from the university colleges, especially the rather posh young ladies who had the opportunity to mingle with a bit of rough. Maybe they gained a bit more knowledge of life from mixing with people from a completely different background to their own. The bar could be quite a rowdy place at times and was eventually closed and locked up by the College authorities. The bar's closure just prompted some of the lads to kick down the door and reopen the bar. After that it stayed open. When I returned last year there was no bar in the basement! A sign of the changes in the College, changes in the law, or just a logical progression?

During my second term at Ruskin I seemed to hit a complete mental block. The focus on such new concepts and ideas, the constant pressure to study and write weekly essays, got to me in a way that is difficult to explain, and perhaps is only explicable by being a mature student, and being subject to these pressures so late in life and without earlier precedents. I found I could not even read the relevant material for a particular week's study. I mentioned this to one of the tutors who suggested that I needed to make a short break in my studies and find some alternative, perhaps more physical way, of occupying my time. I had always been quite physically active as my focus on football and other sports up to now makes clear. However, this more energetic element of my life had almost completely disappeared recently. Would you believe that the answer to my mental block was squash, no not of the orange fruit variety but of the sporting type? I started to play squash and, within days, the mental barriers broke and I was back at study and learning.

After each semester at Ruskin I returned to GKN and took up my old job. This was really important to me since I was now living on my student grant which had meant reducing my income by about 60 per cent while at College, though in part this had been offset by a wonderful gesture by my workmates at GKN. Shortly after arriving in Oxford, I received a letter from one of my fellow shop stewards at GKN. I remember Arthur, for it was he who wrote to me, with great affection as a union colleague and a staunch supporter. His face lives on in my memory simply because he was an advocate or should that be a devotee of Leon Trotsky, and wore a small goatee beard and half-rimmed glasses like his hero. However, despite what the media might think or say about such people, Arthur would have given you the shirt off his back if you had needed it. A real gentleman, though I imagine the media of the time, perhaps even now, would not have looked beyond his politics to identify the real character of the man.

The letter that I received contained a cheque for £7 and the observation that the lads on the shop floor— not just the AUEW boys, but some of the other members of the other main union in the shop, the Screw, Nut, Bolt and Rivets Trade Society—had each agreed to donate two shillings each week and that I would receive £7 a week as a supplement from them. If my mathematics are correct that meant that 70 of my ex-colleagues were willing to contribute. I could not believe their generosity and was going to sent it back but he had written something, and I highlight this because to me it was crucially important.

He wrote, 'One of the attributes of a rounded man is the ability to receive gracefully'. I am not sure if those were his words or a quote from someone else, but they made me weep. He also wrote 'You have earned an enormous amount of goodwill in the shop. You have also given many people a reflected pride and vicarious pleasure in the realisation that some of us at least are capable of breaking the bonds of comparative industrial slavery and moving into the world of further education'. I make no apology for being a wimp and noting that, even now, as I write this it is with tears in my eyes, and that I cherish the letter which is before me right now.

Returning to GKN during the 1965 summer break from Ruskin, I prepared a union claim for a colleague in another mill stressing that he should not use the written claim but use it as the basis for his presentation to his manager. There was nothing too complicated about the claim and it should have caused no problems either for the shop steward or the Company. However, apparently he read directly from the paper and was asked where it had originated. There was nothing dramatic about the claim, it simply used data I had worked through and which I had learned about while at Ruskin College. However, one of the management representatives present stated that only Bill Haywood could have produced that.

Unfortunately, at the time the company was going through a tough time and redundancies were in the air. Whether the case above contributed I still cannot tell but, at 3pm on the Friday afternoon before I was due to return to Ruskin for the second year of the course starting on the following Monday, I was called into the company managing directors office—the big boss not my mill manager—and presented with an ultimatum. This was just before the company offices would be closing down for the weekend at 4.30pm and less than 48 hours before I was due to go back to Ruskin. I was given two options. One, I would not be made redundant because of my seniority but would have to leave Ruskin and return full time to GKN. Two, I could return to Ruskin but would be made redundant as a consequence. Little time for a considered reply but I assume that that was what was intended by the big boss. I had to make a rapid decision and settled for a return to Ruskin.

It was one of the hardest decisions I have ever had to make. I could stay at GKN with all my friends and the generosity they had shown to me, or go back to Ruskin with all that that implied for the future. However, I felt that gaining further knowledge would in the end enable me to make greater contributions to my fellow workers and decided to continue at Ruskin in the expectation that I would find work back at GKN, or at least in the Midlands on completion. This was despite the fact that, at that time Margaret

Thatcher's government was busy decimating the manufacturing base of the British economy and, within a year, unemployment was reaching officially two and a half million and unofficially due to the massaging of the data and the exclusion of certain categories of people, unemployment had risen to an estimated three and a half to four million.

On the following Sunday, after making this decision, I returned to Ruskin with all the uncertainty that involved. By the end of that year, and with the intention of returning to the West Midlands and employment I had sent out nearly two hundred job applications. I received only four responses with two interviews offered and, at both interviews, it was clear that there was a preferred in-house applicant.

My two years at Ruskin were spent in two of the warmest of the decade, and probably for the previous 20 or 30 years, these were the summers of 1975 and 1976. The temperature was frequently in the 80s and 90s and there were days spent studying out on the grass by the Isis or debating in the local riverside hostelries such as the Trout and the Perch. Just outside Oxford, there was a pub called the Bell in Blenheim which served fantastic, reasonably priced food, and this was visited several times over the years. Strangely enough, there were two pubs quite close to each other and both called the Bell. One day I must go back and see if my Bell still exists. Given the huge numbers of old pubs being shut down in recent years they may not have survived.

At Ruskin, I studied Labour Economics and Statistics and obtained distinctions in both, with passes in Industrial Sociology, Industrial Relations and Politics. In addition there were Communications endorsements in Teaching Methods, Public Communication Skills, Public Speaking, and Use of English. Wow, what was it I indicated earlier about not having had a very good education in the English language. Maybe they were just being kind at Ruskin?

In order to complete the course we also had to write a thesis which we researched and completed over one term. Mine was 'A Study of the Hotel and Catering Industry in the West Midlands' and I had to visit a number of hotels, restaurants and pubs to carry out the research, including talking to some of the unions who were engaged in recruitment to the industry. This also included a thorough examination of data from various government and non-government sources regarding the industry. This study for Ruskin College was my first experience of conducting research and I loved it. It was to lead to much of what I did over the following 25 plus years. I guess, in part, this new field of work was due to my curiosity and maybe even because I enjoyed learning new things and exchanging ideas with those being interviewed which might lead to their becoming more efficient in what they did. After all, that was what I had set out to do when going to Ruskin, and for this I had given up full time employment with GKN.

Before leaving the subject of Ruskin College, a short digression on the sinking of a college rowing eight. Was this deliberate, an act of rebellion, or an accident? As it was related at the time, Ruskin possessed a steel-bodied punt. This was taken out on the Isis by two or three of our students who managed to place it in the path of one of the other colleges rowing eights. Result, serious damage to the other colleges rowing eight which cost the College around £2,000 to repair. I am not sure of all the facts since I was not there at the incident, but it sounds reasonable to assume it actually occurred in the way related here.

Oxford contains so many wonderful memory's, mostly it was the College and the people within it, but also the city itself. You could not be there without marvelling at the atmosphere of the place. Despite being a centre of higher education it was also a major industrial employer, in the car industry in particular. In fact, Oxford had been, still is to a certain extent, one of the major car-making centre's in the UK, originally hosting Austin's and Leyland's. Now I believe as the Rover Group or has it changed yet again? Earlier, it had been British Leyland. However, it is difficult to keep up with all the changes that seem to be occurring in the car industry, though I am informed that it is now BMW making Mini's, or did BMW sell to someone else recently? During my time there, Oxford was still very much a place of Town and Gown. I returned to Oxford for several days last year as I noted earlier, and it seemed to be overrun with tourists. You could hardly find a pavement to walk upon. My mind also seemed to have been playing tricks on me for several of the places I had known during the 1974/76 period I seemed unable to locate. Were they gone or just misplaced in my mind?

Had I made the right choice about leaving GKN? Well, inadvertently in many senses I had. That next summer, I believe it was 1976, though it may have been a year later in 1977, GKN closed down the site where I had been working and, which had been involved in manufacturing in the region for over one hundred years. The site was in Heath Street in Smethwick and had been the original site of two companies called Guest and Nettlefold who occupied opposite sides of the same street. Since their products had great synergy they eventually combined and, together with Keen, who joined Guest at an earlier stage, they became the largest engineering company in Britain when they expanded into other areas of production, including measuring instruments, car parts, and military vehicles. At one stage, during the 1960s, GKN employed over 90,000 people, as I noted above, on a worldwide basis but, by far the majority of whom resided in the UK. I believe that the original synergy of the amalgamation of GKN was as I described, though when that occurred escapes me. You will have to forgive an old man's memory and I can't be bothered to delve back into the history of the companies. What was I saying about loving to carry out research? Maybe it is a little late for me to start researching again.

Instead of manufacturing their own product at Heath Street, GKN became a merchandiser importing from the Far East the same type of products they had been making themselves and they closed our factory down. I guess paternalism can only go so far when faced with the prospect of making or losing money. Or was it a simply a case of closing a profitable site in order to make more money by importing cheaper products? Certainly, around that period of time that sort of philosophy existed in the country. For example, many profitable coal mines were being closed down in order to raise overall average profitability in the industry. I am sure many other industries were similarly engaged.

Again, it made me wonder about the plausibility of remaining loyal to any one employer. As I noted earlier, a glance at the football world seems to provide the answer. Many players, managers and owners seem to see the sport as merely one to provide profit for them-selves as they move between clubs at will. Left behind, of course, are the loyal supporters who follow their home clubs through thick and thin and who would rather give up on the game than support an alternative team, especially if that second team was a local one and had been a rival. It has been said that football is a form of tribalism, with close neighbours, such as, West Bromwich Albion and Aston Villa, Liverpool and Everton, and especially Glasgow Rangers and Celtic, being examples of this. Actually, there is more than an element of truth in this belief.

You note I said above supporter's 'home team'. Nowadays, many youngsters seem to support only the richest and most successful teams. No longer do they seem to feel an affinity with their local clubs, who are perhaps unable to compete with the wealth generated from millionaires, perhaps even billionaires, who have invaded the game in the UK—and more particularly England. Manchester United, I note, have just won, in 2012, yet another Premiership title. Actually, I find this monopoly of the top levels of English football by an elite group of clubs a complete and utter turn-off.

For me it holds no comparison to a time when 22 teams battled it out each season to top what was the First Division of English football. Currently you can forget about fifteen or sixteen of the twenty teams competing for the league title. They are only there as fodder for the four or five teams with a chance of winning the title through their enormous financial advantages. How typical is this of society in general in the UK!

It is also unfortunate that it appears that sportsmanship and fair play have almost completely disappeared from the professional game. Cheating has now become endemic and this spreads down to the lower levels. One newspaper commentator recently made the comment that he no longer felt there were anything other than cheats left in professional football. It seemed to be expected that in order to compete, one had to cheat. This has been echoed by at least one senior Premiership manager, who I refrain from naming, though his claim did appear in the newspapers. Cheating seemed to be encouraged and this was justified by winning.

You will find repeated comments on sportsmanship in this book. I cannot help it, it is my passion. Players claiming dubious penalties and corners, diving at the slightest provocation, pulling shirts, sneaking five, ten and more yards for throw-ins and fouls while the referee's back is turned, occur in every match. This is justified by some ex-professional footballers, who appear on television as commentators, as merely the will to win. They will justify fouls as being 'professional'. Sorry, a foul is a foul, is a foul, is a foul. No distinction for me. You abide by the rules or you do not. I think it would be rather nice to see referees from rugby union or rugby league take control of football matches. You might find that matches have to be abandoned, because there are not enough players left on the pitch to continue having been sent off for infringements of the rules!

Are we teaching children that only money and success are desirable in our modern world? Again I refer to Margaret Thatcher, who it seems to me, promoted the concept of self before society. Are current Coalition objectives that much different? Thatcher, together with her economist guru Professor Alan Walters, advocated the concept of 'trickle down', e.g. if you let the people at the top of the pile make as much money as they can this will trickle down to the lower levels of society. What a load of old cobblers! It did not work then and certainly does not work now, even though the Coalition, at least most of them, seem to think it does. This concept on their part is not too surprising, given that so many of them are excessively wealthy.

In modern times, this concept of selfishness and greed seems increasingly obvious. Footballers reach out for increased contracts even where they already receive what some would call obscene amounts of money. Bankers screw society and each other to get as much money for them-selves as they can. Unfortunately, successive governments have allowed this to occur.

Now we find out that many of the international companies making billions of pounds from the British economy pay miniscule amounts of tax to the Treasury. While large sums of money are paid out by the government to catch so-called 'scroungers' in society little attempt is made to make such companies pay a fair share of their profits to Her Majesty's Revenue and Customs (HMRC), and thus to the ordinary tax payer. When they are caught with their hands in the till, if they are caught, they very often negotiate with HMRC and pay only miniscule amounts of the taxes they should have paid to the revenue.

Similarly, owners, managers, directors treat the sport of football as more of a business than a sport. As noted above, the only loyal people associated with the game are the supporters, and they are frequently treated with contempt by their team. Recent developments have revealed that some of the most highly paid sportsmen and women, along with others in the entertainment industry, are actually paid through off-shore companies thus reducing their income tax liabilities. Glasgow Rangers have recently been accused of this and surely they are not the only ones. How about stopping that little tax evasion game? I know it's called avoidance rather than evasion but what is in a name? One way you are a cheat, the other way you're 'canny', and that's justifiable?

I recall something I read in one newspaper that, on visiting one restaurant a particular, very well known footballer, was giving his waiter quite a lot of verbal abuse. The reporter noted that, that particular footballer received more in one week in terms of salary, said to be over £150,000 a week, than the waiter could earn in seven or more years. You will note I said the footballer received, not earned! Now, I understand that under current renegotiation of his contract he could receive upwards of £200,000 per week!

Axe firmly ground and its back to discussing the results of being at Ruskin and what followed. On completing my Diploma course, I was unemployed despite the many job applications that I had made in the interim and I did the only thing left open to me, I applied for a Bachelor of Arts (BA) degree at university

BILL HAYWOOD

where I could still at least obtain a grant to keep me going.

I applied to Sussex University who had a very open attitude to mature students and, having been accepted registered for an Economics BA degree. In part as a result of my Ruskin Diploma I was accepted, and in October 1976, moved onto campus to live amongst students half my age, and to start my Economics degree. Given my Ruskin experience I was excused the introductory first year of the degree and went straight into the second year. This was both a plus and a minus. A plus because it meant a two-year degree instead of three, and a minus because I missed one element of the Economics degree and went in cold to the second year. From then on, I was playing catch-up.

I moved on to campus to live in Kent House. Even though this was an academic environment, it had echoes of the RAF. There were separate individual rooms but I was, in some sense, once more living in a communal environment complete with a shared kitchen on each floor. Fortunately, within a few months, I was able to find accommodation off campus and become more able to enjoy the pubs and social life of Brighton, not that I had a great deal of money to do so.

If I felt like the daddy at Ruskin, here I felt like the granddaddy. My fellow intake were all under 20 years old and by now I was 38 years old! Fortunately, on my first day at the university I entered a lift that had two tutors in. One commented *"Thank god I have two mature students in my group. At least they will keep things going"*. It turned out that while for those two tutors this may have been spoken in jest, it proved to be correct in at least one case where I was concerned. During one session, towards the end of my second term we were in a 30-student discussion group debating Microeconomics. We had had small group meetings with personal tutors, lectures from the high and mighty of the profession, and had probably spent at least 50 hours discussing and reading about profit maximising, product maximising, satisficing, and so on and so on.

The tutor opened up by saying how long we had been looking at these concepts over the previous two or three weeks and what did we all think about them? He leaned his chair back against the wall and looked around. Deadly silence, being the only 'aged' person present I had in the past tended to open my mouth more readily than the rest of the intake but now I thought 'Keep your mouth shut and let's see if anyone else has the nerve to commit themselves' The silence continued for several minutes and the tutor, Julian, looked at me and smiled. The silence continued. Eventually it became apparent that he was likely to spend the next two hours waiting for a response.

I eventually broke the silence. *"Julian"*, I said, *"Profit/ Product maximisation is a lovely concept but having worked in industry for well over ten years it's a load of twaddle. It is not how managers I have known operate"*, (though I did not use the word 'twaddle'). I stressed that, if any of the concepts we had worked on was at all relevant and that was somewhat doubtful, it was *'satisfying'*, managing for the most effective and efficient outcome at the very local level, e.g. at shop floor level. In general, I just felt that there was little or no overall target in most of the companies I had worked for. Each department strove for its own results in the hope that they would perform better than the other managers in the firm.

That broke the ice and we spent two hours on the topic. I believe one other student sort of half agreed with me but most were advocates of profit maximising, so much for book learning. It seemed as though only the reading materials had impacted on the students' minds. Most of my fellow students had probably done nothing more than a paper round or worked as a minor part of their parents', or their parents' friends enterprises. Perhaps working for a living on the shop floor had its advantages in the academic world after all. At the end of the session Julian said, *"Well, of course we have to learn about all these concepts and how they are supposed to work. But, at the end of the day, I believe Bill summed it up best at the beginning as a load of b***s, but you have to learn it to pass your exams"*.

One small digression here about living on the Sussex University campus during those early months, one dark winter's evening, having worked until about 9pm in my room during my first term while resident on campus, I decided to walk up to the Swan Inn in Falmer for a quick pint. I noticed that their guest ale was something which was called Theakston's Old Peculier. I had heard of this and decided to try a pint. Upon asking for it I was asked if I really wanted a full pint and I said yes. It was great, and soon a second pint was ordered. The pub was run by an elderly lady and, by this, I mean well into her eighties. She was very strict about closing time. Ten minutes exactly was allowed after the official 10.30 closing time, just time for another quick half pint before having to leave and go back down the hill to campus. Leaving the pub, the street outside was completely dark, no street lighting at all in this part of the village at that time. No problem, I felt as sober as a judge—who ever decided that judges were ever 'sober' maybe they disregarded alcohol as a condition? Suddenly, as I walked down the street, I noticed that the white line down the middle of the road which I was following in the dark seemed to be moving from side to side. Drunk on two and a half pints of beer consumed in just over one hour!.

While living on campus, I became good friends with a young lady named Anne who was a little older than the average student, being in her early 20s.

We occasionally went out for meals together in the evenings, and at times lounging out on the grass chatting and drinking Martini's together in the sunshine—not shaken or stirred—just Dry Martini, ice and slice, with lemonade! James Bond, eat your heart out. Wow, this certainly beat eating sandwiches and playing football on the local canal bank during our lunch hour when I worked at Phillips Cycles.

Anne could be quite feisty when aroused and, after having moved off campus to move in with a female friend, she often went across the road to the local pub, The Shakespeare's Head, where she spent some time drinking on her own and being spoken to by no one. Shortly afterwards, a room became available in that same house and I moved in with Anne and her friend. Such a relief to get off campus and back into something akin to the real world, and two nights after moving in, I accompanied Anne to that same pub and, within minutes, we were chatting to the locals. On returning to the house, she blew her top. Not at me but at the people in the pub. She had been ignored when on her own but accepted because she was with me. Perhaps, before, she had been seen as a potential problem not as a happy young lady who enjoyed the odd bevvy.

By the third term I had moved yet again, this time into a rented basement apartment in Kemptown, a suburb of Brighton and one which had almost a village feel to it. In fact, it is called a village by the local populace. At last an apartment of my own. Kemptown was a wonderful place to live, friendly and with lots of things to do plus great local pubs selling a range of wonderful real ales: Harvey's which was brewed nearby in Lewes, Gales, and King and Barnes beers, and many others. It was a beer drinker's paradise.

For a while—I think it was about seven months—I was able to earn a little extra money, £5 a session, by working behind the bar in the Stag's Head pub in Kemptown. The Stag was the second oldest pub in Brighton and, when the coach and horse had been the normal mode of transport between London and Brighton, it had been the final staging inn for the area. The Stag was only a small pub but, from opening time to closing time, it was packed because of the quality of the beer. Coach parties, of the motorised variety rather than the horse-drawn, came fairly often bearing members of the Campaign for Real Ale (CAMRA). This was a bit weird for, often, they would stay for only about an hour, crowding out the place given that the pub only had one small bar, a small games room (i.e. a dart board and a small Space Invaders machine) and what was termed as 'the snug', a room with one or two small tables as I recall, and these connoisseurs of beer normally only drank a couple of half pints each.

I pointed out to the owner, Bill, that, together, these 30 or so people drank only about 30 pints between them while filling the place and excluding other potential customers from entry given that, as noted above, it was at that time a very small pub (since enlarged following its take-over by another company of course!). Bill loved the attention that CAMRA gave to the pub until I pointed out that Harry, Frank and Charlie, three old timers who usually arrived a little after six o'clock, and stayed until nearly 11pm, sat in the snug and drank about two or three pints an hour each, for just over four hours. In other words these three old timers drank something in the region of 30 pints between them, about as much as all the CAMRA buffs put together!

Bill had a policy of only employing bar staff for a month or two, his reasoning being that, after that, petty pilfering became endemic. Since at that time I only lived a few hundred yards from the pub I always arrived at the bar with not a penny in my pockets. If challenged, there was no way I could be accused of pilfering, but he never asked, and as I noted above I lasted there for seven months before Bill sold the place, and moved to the Isle of Wight where he purchased a thatched-cottage style pub with rooms to let, after first selling the Stag for a considerable profit.

Over the next two years at Sussex University on the Economics BA I explored Macro- and Microeconomics, Statistics, Industrial Sociology, Labour Economics, Philosophy and so on, and so on. In the three hour exams at the end of the course I got by, managing Lower Seconds and Third Class marks. However, the extended paper's completed over several days or longer were all Upper Seconds. A lot can be said for having time to think through problems and working them out for yourself. Perhaps that was one advantage that being an older age gave me. I ended up, at the end of the course with a 2:2 degree. Maybe with that extra year I might have managed a 2:1 but it was not that important to me. A job was!

However, still no jobs after a further 400 applications and now the employment situation out there was even worse. What to do? Well, I was coming to the end of the year and eligible for more statutory funding so how about a Master of Science (MSc) degree in the History and Social Studies of Science (HSSS) course at the Mantell Building, again at Sussex University. One of the BA Economics courses had been taught by a brilliant Professor by the name of Chris Freeman and I really took to it, possibly because it entailed more about researching. Chris was the head of the Science Policy Research Unit (SPRU) in the Mantell Building, and they were closely involved as a dual partner with HSSS in the course I hoped to take. Initially, when I was accepted for the course, HSSS was the home centre for both the MSc and DPhil courses they ran together with SPRU. SPRU, however, was not able to accept its own students' at that time but they were, and still are, a leading research group and the research element of the MSc course really appealed to me.

The HSSS course intake was comprised equally of students from the UK and overseas, sixteen students in all: eight from the UK and eight international students. Half of each group had a first degree in the Arts and the other half in the Sciences. This turned out to be a really stimulating, and demanding, mix of people. We had South and North Americans on the course, Chinese, East Europeans and Japanese amongst others.

Each term, we were given two different elements to study. I think that, like my time at Ruskin, one element of the HSSS course that pushed me to the limit of my abilities, was the Philosophy element in the second term. I hope that you can appreciate that we were faced with others in the group who all had a first degree in a particular subject. In this term, we had two students who were Philosophy graduates. After two weeks, I approached the tutor and explained that I would no longer attend the joint seminars because of the dominance of one person in particular. I felt that I was not learning anything from these meetings because of his dominance, perhaps the tutor could have managed the meetings a little more firmly and given more direction. I stressed that I wished to continue with the course on my own with his guidance and the use of the recommended reading. He agreed. However, one of the results of experiencing the tutor's lack of control of the group was that I eventually took a much firmer control myself in later years when this was needed.

At the beginning of the Philosophy course we had each been allocated a subject on which we as individuals would be leaders. Mine was 'Incommensurability'. Wow. I could barely spell it and had no clue what it meant or involved. Course reading included Kuhn, Popper, Lakatos and Feyerabend, amongst others.

I got through that term by concentrating almost exclusively on the Philosophy element and, at the end of the course, was awarded a 2:1 mark. The other element being studied during that term was Industrial Sociology, that by now was something I was quite good at, I achieved a 2:2. I guess that proves how much I was determined to succeed at something I knew nothing about, to the detriment of something that I did know something about.

Well, the year passed and I achieved my MSc from HSSS to go with my BA in Economics. What to do now? There was still mass unemployment in the country and more job applications had been sent out during the term and still there was no potential for employment. The two job interviews I did manage to be offered had been made with the same result as the earlier ones during my Ruskin Diploma and my BA course. It seemed that I had educated myself out of the type of jobs I had previously had and was being viewed with suspicion by employers in the types of industry from which I had emerged. I was also viewed as too old for what I shall term as employment in the educational sector, where starting salaries were geared to 20 year olds.

I was 41 years old and, at this stage, seemed fitted for neither industry nor education. I did the only thing left to me. I had one year of funding available to me from statutory sources. I registered with HSSS again this time for a Doctor of Philosophy (DPhil) degree, with a view that I would take any job available during the latter part of the degree in order to support myself. By the time I finished the doctoral degree, five years later, SPRU had been authorised to take its own students. As a result I believe I may have been the first person to receive a degree awarded through SPRU, though I received this *in absentia*. The thought of cap and gown was a real turn-off, though in later years, I thought that my sister Edna might have liked me to have attended for the doctoral ceremony so she could see this but by then it was too late, the decision had been made. Maybe I was too selfish about what I felt was important to me, myself, and had disregarded what others may have wished for me. I guess I have always been rather selfish in this way. Again, a little later I explain this selfishness more fully. All three of my degrees were obtained thus, through the post. My Ruskin Diploma and my three University degrees now reside in an old, tattered and torn, brown A4 envelope in my bedside table.

In seeking supervision for the DPhil, I struck very lucky indeed. I asked Professor Freeman if he would act as my supervisor and he agreed. It shows the humility of this man that he actually thanked me for asking him. If the word genius applied to anyone I had ever encountered up till then, it did to Chris Freeman, and I am not sure I have met anyone since who measures up to a similar accolade.

The topic I chose for my doctoral thesis was 'Technical Change and Employment in the British Printing Industry'. Printing is the second oldest profession and originated in a more formal sense with the development of the Gutenburg Press over 500 years ago, though the Chinese were printing using clay tablets 2000 years ago. Did I hear anyone query what the oldest profession was? Well, the first is said to be occupied by the gloriously named ladies of the night!

In the 1970s, the printing industry was undergoing a revolution in its processes, particularly at the front end in the technology movement. The normal and established printing processes were letterpress, lithographic, flexographic, gravure and screen printing systems, which had been used for many years. New computerized photo-composing pre-press systems and modern presses and finishing systems, were now being installed with the consequence that employment levels and skills were rapidly changing. Many of the old skills associated with letterpress, lithography and gravure in particular, were being impacted in a major way. Jobs were being lost and/or de-skilled, yet many of these expensive new systems were being under utilised and/or plain poorly utilised.

People tend to equate the printing industry with newspapers and particularly with high wages and union militancy. Wrong. The newspaper sector comprised a very small part of the printing industry at that time, perhaps six or seven per cent of those employed in printing, worked in it. By far the largest group of workers was employed within the general printing sector, at that time comprising somewhere around 70 per cent or more of total employment in the trade. Unionisation was also far lower outside of the newspaper industry, as were salaries.

During the five years it took to complete the doctorate, I developed and distributed over 200 questionnaires to printers in various areas of the industry and throughout Britain. I also visited approximately a hundred companies to discuss the use of their manufacturing processes, how they saw themselves developing further, what skills they had or required, and what forms of training they offered. In addition I had a second questionnaire which was addressed to equipment suppliers to the industry. Over 50 companies were contacted and 30 interviews carried out in such companies. A third element of the research involved the workforce and their representatives. Many of the companies I visited, both printers and equipment suppliers, allowed me access to their employees to discuss how they felt about the changes taking place and whether they were happy with developments. Not all were, but it shows the openness of some employers that they allowed such access.

In addition, I interviewed many union representatives, including those at the highest level in the National Graphical Association (NGA), the Society of Lithographic Artists, Designers, Engravers and Process Workers (SLADE), the Society of Graphical and Allied Trades (SOGAT), the National Society of Operative Printers, Graphical and Media Personnel (NATSOPA) and the National Society of Journalists (NUJ). It has to be noted that hardly any of these unions exist today in the same form that they did then because of combination with other bodies, either in the printing industry itself or by amalgamation with the more powerful general unions.

Interviews were conducted with companies ranging from five employees through to 1,500. The British Printing Corporation in Bristol and run by the infamous Robert Maxwell—who I interviewed personally—was the largest, and this went right through to a small printer in Crawley who it took me three months to persuade to see me. I badgered this man for all of those three months before he agreed to spare me twenty minutes. When I finally met with this small printer, he found that I was someone who did not approach his industry as an academic because of my industrial background. He had been concerned about wasting his time with an academic but found that I had a genuine interest in learning about his company and exchanging ideas. When the interview finally took place it lasted three and a half hours!

As I noted earlier, it took five years to complete the doctorate. Half of the second year was spent trying to raise funds to continue the doctorate full time. I approached numerous organisations involved with research from an academic standpoint and even the research funding bodies. Eventually I was successful by gaining funding from the Technical Change Centre (TCC) in London, a reasonably new organisation run by Sir Bruce Williams as a counterpoint to the Science Policy Research Unit, run by Chris Freeman. This gave me funds for the second year but it entailed working for them for the next year.

The draft of the thesis was initially completed by being written in about seven weeks over the Christmas period in 1984/5, though by then having worked for TCC for almost the stipulated one year I had moved on from there to employment with Brighton Polytechnic, who were eventually to become the University of Brighton. We were on Christmas vacation from the Polytechnic for three weeks, plus I took an additional four week annual holiday in order to write up the thesis. After each chapter was completed, I dropped it off to Chris Freeman to look at and comment on, then ploughed on with the next chapter.

The rather amazing thing in compiling the thesis was that I had gathered an enormous amount of material during the preceding five years which had filled a four-drawer steel cabinet. This was full of completed questionnaires and much more other material collected over the years. I hardly looked into its contents. It seemed that most of what I wanted to write was stuck up there in my head. I believe that this was why the thesis was completed so rapidly. Occasionally, I had to dig into the cabinet but on surprisingly few occasions. The thesis was completed with rewrites following comments from Chris, I think it was in May 1985. In total, I ended up with a roughly 400-page thesis produced on an old Apple computer and printed on an old daisy wheel printer.

The oral examination of the thesis was conducted by my supervisor Chris Freeman and Roy Moore from Ruskin College, Oxford. The third member of the panel was Professor Roy Rothwell, a highly regarded and respected academic who sadly died the following year. At the end of the oral examination, I was asked to make a couple of minor changes but, subject to these, was given an outright pass. I was now a Doctor of Philosophy, and as I noted above the doctoral degree, together with my BA, MSc and Social Studies Diploma from Ruskin now reside in that tattered old brown A4 envelope in my bedside cupboard. I never could understand why people wanted to frame and display these items.

It was shortly after completing the doctorate that I became an external tutor for the Open University (OU) MSc course on technical change. Over the following three years, I acted as tutor to ten OU mature students nine of whom obtained their degrees following the preparation and submission of their theses. One dropped out and failed to complete the course. Having been a mature student myself helped me to understand the problems these students faced in holding down jobs, while studying for their degrees in their spare time. One student in particular, was a woman who was travelling about thirty miles each way, daily, to hold down a job, while simultaneously running a home and caring for three children, while at the same time studying in the evenings. She evoked great admiration in me, and I am happy to say her thesis when finally submitted was highly regarded by her OU administrators, and she successfully obtained her MSc.

I think that possibly this was one of the most satisfying areas of my work since leaving GKN, and I had turned the full circle from being a mature student myself, to assisting others in their development, something I have striven for since the start of my academic career.

Out of full time education and into employment

As a consequence of my commitment to the Technical Change Centre, and because I still lived in Brighton, the London job involved getting up at about 6am in order to get over to the railway station to catch the London train at 7.10am. Arriving at Victoria Station just after 8am, it was onto the underground and onwards to Kensington High Street tube station. In the office by 8.30am, work till 5.15pm, hang around until the rush hour had ended and back on a train to Brighton at approximately 7pm. A meal was consumed by about 8.30pm or so, a couple of beers in my local pub, the Wellington at the bottom of the street, and back to bed by 11 or 11.30pm to start the whole process once more for five days a week. The cost of travel up and down between Brighton and London was prohibitive, even at that time. My salary at the Technical Change Centre was a little under £9,000 a year gross and the annual season ticket to London on the train was over £1,000, about 15% of my nett income if my memory serves me correctly.

I was still living with an overdraft and saw little chance of reducing it during this period and while still living in digs. The travel, the financial uncertainty and the overall stress levels were high but fortunately did not last too long. For that second year of the doctorate, I had worked with Professor Ed Sciberras at the TCC and he eventually left at the end of that year, to return to an appointment in his native Australia, I believe it was the University of Woolongong. This gave me the opportunity to leave the Technical Change Centre— with Sir Bruce's permission—and take a job I had been offered at Brighton Polytechnic with Professor John Bessant.

The salary at the Polytechnic was more or less the same as that at the TCC but, of course, I had no major travel expenses so more was left for other purposes. Slightly more money, less expense and just around the corner from where I was soon to buy my first ever property, so I did not need my own transport. At last, I was able to start paying off some of the debt I had accumulated over the years. And at last I was able to start to get something of a normal social life, while still managing to work on both the Polytechnic work with John and my own doctorate.

It was around this time, in the mid 1980s, that I even managed to buy that first property. Can you imagine moving towards 50 years old and my own flat and mortgage for the very first time! Actually I was 48 years old then and the mortgage was for 22 years and was to last until I was 70 years old! The flat I bought was on Bear Road, right opposite the cemetery. Only a half a mile stroll from my office at the Polytechnic so no more expensive travel arrangements. A regular bus service down into town, and a bus stop right outside my front door, so no need for a car and all the expense that that might entail.

Brighton was both enjoyable and a potential danger at that time, not sure about now. Brighton is a stimulating place to live—and I loved being by the sea—always have done and this is why I now live very close to the coast here in Cyprus and within view of the Mediterranean. However, there was a certain element of risk associated with Brighton in those days. In the evenings you could wander into areas where crime was rife and I believe that, percentage-wise there are, or were at that time, more murders per head of population in Brighton than there were in London. Brighton is actually called by many 'London by the Sea' and many celebrities lived in Brighton, particularly in the arts world of music and theatre, since living in Brighton and working in London was very convenient for them.

It was around this time that I started playing darts for my local pub, the Newmarket Arms on Bear Road. Did we have a team! Several players of county standard were included and we cleaned up both the league and cup competitions. Now, I know there are people out there saying 'Why write about boring old darts!' Well you would be amazed by how many people enjoy the sport so, if your not interested, let it pass you by.

By the way, watching darts now on television is a complete turn off for me. All that razzamatazz that now occurs, the shouting, and the booing is anathema to me. When I played you expected, and got, silence when you were at the oche. Now, like much else in the sporting world, it's not the sport that is important but the fact that its 'showbiz' and people wanting to get their face on television. I was pretty good at darts and actually ended up at the end of the season with the highest win average in our team, something in the region of 94 per cent, besides which, it is a pleasant way to pass a couple of hours while supping a nice pint of beer. Similarly, there were pub Crib leagues. I played for the Newmarket at that as well and we also won cups in that competition too. Life is not just about work—its the ability to remove yourself for a while from the merry-go-round of work that makes the work more pleasurable.

The work with John Bessant was quite complementary with my continuing doctorate, which I was able to carry on with in my own time. John and I were looking at the Computer Integration of Technologies (CIM) in what were termed Flexible Manufacturing Systems (FMS). This involved the integration of machine tools and transfer systems under the control of computerised technology. I managed a large part of the project, arranging interviews with over 100 companies and, in most cases, carrying out the interviews myself, using an adapted version of the questionnaire I had developed originally for my print industry research. Numerous publications ensued and I attended many conferences and seminars and, made a number of presentations myself.

During this time, I travelled fairly extensively all over Europe, including Germany, Italy, Belgium, Austria and France, and into Northern Europe to Sweden, Norway, Denmark and Finland. I seemed to be flying out of, or into, mainly Gatwick, but occasionally Heathrow every two or three weeks. Over later years, and all related to conducting research or the diffusion of research to other interested parties, I also visited Poland, Hungary, the then Czechoslovakia, now of course, the Czech and Slovak Republics, the USA, Brazil, Mauritius, and many other places.

A number of these trips stand out in my mind. One was to a conference in Finland. I took a flight to Helsinki and stayed overnight in a hotel in order to catch an early morning flight up to Ivalo in the North of Finland. Helsinki is on the Southern coast and Ivalo is near the Northern coast. I seem to recall the internal flight took over an hour, perhaps two, the memory isn't as good as it was? Finland is a big country, with Ivalo being located about twenty kilometres from both the border with what was then the Soviet Union to the East, and from the Arctic Circle to the North, or so I was informed. The conference was held in what was used as a ski lodge during winter but this was early July. The temperature was around 90 degrees and very humid. One evening, we were taken out on a boat on what was said to be the largest lake in Finland, of which Finland was said to have a thousand. At 11.45pm, I took a photograph of the sun dipping down to the horizon. At midnight we had stopped at a small island and I climbed to the top and took a second photograph, with the tip of the sun just visible on the horizon. That photograph is one of the images contained in this book, though in black and white rather than the original colour. Back on the boat and, at a quarter past twelve, I took a third photograph which revealed the sun rising again. I had those photographs blown up to poster size and framed. They adorn my walls here in Cyprus.

On another evening, I left the hotel and took a stroll around the chalets. Turning one corner, I was confronted by the most enormous animal I have ever got close to. Standing stock still, ten feet in front of me was what I took to be a moose or caribou or some such. It certainly did not look like a reindeer, of which there were so many locally. This animal looked bigger than a shire horse from where I stood, looking up into its face. Its antlers were several feet across and very broad. We stood and stared at each other for a short while, with neither of us moving. Very slowly I sidled backwards around the corner and strolled rapidly back to the ski lodge.

It was while at Ivalo that I encountered the worst case of mosquito bites that I have experienced anywhere in the world. It seemed incredible but, here in the far North of Finland, there are about five different varieties of mosquito, or so I was later told. They range from ones you could barely see to ones that seemed to be as big as ordinary house flies. Visiting a Sami (Finnish Eskimo) encampment one evening, we were advised to take clothing that covered most of our skin because of these insects. I wore a light waterproof jacket with a hood that had elasticated sleeves which I pulled down over my hands and with the hood up and tied around my neck. My trousers were tucked into my socks. I can honestly say I was not aware of being bitten during the evening as we sat eating reindeer stew but, when I returned to the hotel at midnight, and because of the humidity and the enclosing clothing, I stripped off and took a shower. All around my wrists, my ankles and even my waist were rings of mosquito bites. I counted about fifty before I gave up counting. How the hell they got through my clothing I will never now. It took nearly six months until those red rings of bites gradually and finally faded.

Other visits that stand out in my mind were the two I made to Mauritius. Britain had colonised Mauritius after throwing out the French over a hundred years before but I found many of the businesses that I visited were run by Frenchmen and Frenchwomen who could trace their Mauritian ancestry back for a couple of centuries, or more. Mauritius also seemed to be one of the most successfully integrated societies I have ever come across. Technically, Mauritius is in Sub-Saharan Africa though many hundreds of miles from the African continent. However, the Mauritian population comes from all over the World—Africa, India, Britain, France and China—and at that time there seemed to be no signs of disputes between the national ethnic groups. Long may that continue. The Chinese population, in particular, had grown rapidly around the time of my visits in the early 1990s. The influx of Chinese was because of the shortly due return of Hong

Kong from British to Chinese rule, when many Hong Kong Chinese were leaving to go to Mauritius or other places.

Halfway through my time at Brighton Polytechnic we became Brighton University. This did not make a great deal of difference to our way of working but I guess it added somewhat to the prestige of the institution. In some senses, it probably aided both my own doctoral research and the project research since, when companies or individuals were contacted they seemed more impressed when you revealed you were from a university rather than a polytechnic, though I cannot conceive of why that should be. Eventually, the doctorate did not hurt either during contacts with companies! Not that I think it made a scrap of difference to the quality of the research in either case.

Earlier in this life of Brian, I mentioned being seconded away from Brighton University. This was largely due to the work that John Bessant and myself had been conducting in the UK on computer integrated manufacturing, specifically, flexible manufacturing systems. In January 1990, I was offered a research post at the International Institute for Applied Systems Analysis (IIASA) in Laxenburg, Austria. In part, this involved being co-editor of a series of books bringing together a whole range of national specialists from around the world dealing with computer integrated manufacturing, on which I had become something of a specialist. Four books were eventually published by Chapman and Hall of London and, I was co-editor of three of these books.

Although each chapter of these books was given to me in English, in order to carry out this editing successfully I had to be familiar with both the technical aspects of each chapter and also with exactly what the author was trying to get across. Japanese written English, Scandinavian written English and East European written English are not the most explicit, logical or lucid in the world, or it was not in this case, and I have already noted my own deficiencies in the language. However, we got there and the publications followed.

In addition to the editorial responsibilities I also managed and organised a major international conference which drew experts from around the world including America, Japan, the whole of Europe including Scandinavia and most of Eastern Europe. The conference proved to be a huge success which I was privileged to chair. This is where my earlier experiences with the less than commanding tutor on the Philosophy course at Sussex University, came into play. I had beside me three coloured cards and control of the microphone. I explained to each presenter that they had ten minutes to make their presentation, and that three minutes from the end, I would slide a green card in front of them. Two minutes to go and they got an orange card. One minute to go, a red card. I stressed that at the end of that minute I would switch off the microphone, I am not sure to this day whether I would have had the nerve to do this given the importance of those presenters, but not one presenter ran over his specified time.

This conference brought forward another piece of editing since I had to take each contributor's presentation and bring together a 500 page conference proceedings publication 'CIM: Revolution in Progress', again, with some measure of success. The proceedings were those of the 'Final IIASA Conference on Computer Integrated Manufacturing'.

As a result of my twenty-month secondment to IIASA, I was offered a five-month consultancy as a senior research fellow with the United Nations Industrial Development Organisation (UNIDO) at the Vienna International Centre. The project, which I led, was funded by a Finnish Government development body and was worth $500,000 American dollars. The work was carried out under the umbrella of IIASA. The project involved looking at 'Trends in Industrial

Automation' in seven developing countries, primarily from Africa. The six African countries were Ethiopia, Kenya, Mauritius, Namibia, Tanzania and Zimbabwe. A study of Brazil was selected as a more highly developed comparator. As the project manager, I was responsible for its organisation and report writing. I also personally carried out the research in Mauritius which, as noted above, I visited twice, and in Brazil where I spent a month visiting companies in the Sao Paolo and Rio de Janeiro regions.

A research programme co-worker, Dr Pentti Vuorinen from Finland, carried out research in four other countries Ethiopia, Kenya, Tanzania and Zimbabwe, and a third colleague who worked for UNIDO made contributions in one country, Namibia, while there on other business. Our secretary was of Austro-Hungarian heritage, Ms Eva Toth-Hizsnyik. All of this research was carried out using a slightly revised version of the original questionnaire developed for my doctoral thesis.

Brazil was another country, like Malta, where the differences between the haves and have-nots was quite stark. It is a remarkably beautiful country where, as I noted above, I visited both Rio de Janeiro and Sao Paolo and managed to enjoy the scenery while being conflicted by the social differences I could see about me. In Rio, the hotel room I was allocated was at the rear of the building and overlooked a little valley but, within what seemed like just a few hundred yards, and on the side of a hill was a favela. These are quite primitive groups of buildings, built mostly of tin and bits of wood and is where the more deprived people of Rio live. I understand the police only go in there mob-handed and with guns drawn.

On the street outside the hotel, and leading down to the sea, all of the buildings, some of which were residential others being business properties, either had iron railings or strong plate glass windows behind which lurked armed guards. Outside these buildings, and on the pavements people very often just lay around on cardboard boxes or were seeking money from passers-by. These were many of the most unfortunate people of Rio. It will be interesting to see if they are around during the football World Cup in 2014 or the Olympics to be held there soon, and whether the favela's are still so obvious. It was so sad to see, such beauty and such poverty, lingering side by side on the streets of Rio.

One not very amusing escapade that I was involved in occurred on the Copacabana seafront. As I was strolling along, a boy of about 10 kept pointing at my shoes and clearly wanted to polish them, a bit superfluous given I had on trainers. He persisted and, on looking down, saw what appeared to be a lump of grease on my trainer. I sat down on a bench and he started work on the trainer. Just then, two men strolled up one of whom appeared from his speech to be of German origin, his companion a Brazilian. One of them said *"Are you German, English, American?"* I nodded and that yes I was English. *"The boy he offered to clean your shoes, yes?"* Again I nodded. He said, *"The boy sits in the gutter and flicks grease onto people's shoes as they pass, which gives him an excuse to clean them. Do not look around but on the corner behind you there is a young man who when you pull out your money to pay the boy, he will run over and try to snatch your money. If you try to resist he will probably stab you"* So saying, he almost screamed at the boy and took a flying kick at his shoe box, sending it shattered in pieces across the road. I quickly looked around and saw the youth he mentioned scurrying away up the street. Together, we popped into the nearest bar and spent a couple of hours chatting and having a few beers and, just in case you were questioning their motives, no it was not me buying all the beer—they insisted on buying their rounds.

However, to return to the UNIDO story, fortunately I had developed a number of contacts internationally through my time at Ruskin College, where there were

ON LIFE'S LITTLE TWISTS AND TURNS

a number of African colleagues in my intake who had become senior personnel in their own countries following on from their time at Ruskin; and also through my time at the Science Policy Research Unit (SPRU); and during my earlier work with IIASA. All of these many contacts assisted me considerably in setting-up and organising interviews in all the involved countries. It's quite surprising how many useful contacts can be made and how these assist dramatically in setting up interviews, and in arranging travel and accommodation around these countries. The UNIDO project was completed within the scheduled time frame and under budget. A report of over 400 pages was presented to UNIDO within three months and highly rated. Several other publications also resulted.

It would seem from the above that my time in Vienna was dominated by work. That would be incorrect. Though the work was enjoyable and perhaps the most pleasurable of my researcher life there were many more personal and pleasurable things to recall. My time in Austria was notable not for just the work that was entailed. Vienna itself is a beautiful city with many parks and fine buildings. The building in Laxenburg where I worked for over two years for IIASA and UNIDO was actually the summer palace of the late Empress Maria Theresia. Again, a photograph of the palace and its accompanying park are included, but again in black and white rather than in colour. A large park had been created behind the palace complete with a lake and an island with mini castle. I understand that the royal children were rowed out to the castle most days in order to get them out from under the feet of the royal adults. No fishing was allowed in the lake at that time, that was the early 1990s, so close to the bank and just below the surface, swam some of the largest fish I had ever seen.

The office I shared with two colleagues was huge with almost a floor-to-ceiling ornate mirror and huge chandelier. My colleagues were from the Soviet Union which was in the early stages of breaking up, and Finland. The Soviet colleague was Yuri Tchijov and, sadly, he died from a heart attack just three months after my arrival in Austria. Yuri was a very affable and gregarious man who was sadly missed. I think the Finnish colleague went by the name of Jari Mieskonen, but I may be wrong there.

During the Second World War, the palace had been occupied by Soviet troops and had been badly mistreated. Paintings and chandeliers had been destroyed and woodwork torn down for fires. A considerable effort had been made to restore the building and, by the time I arrived, the restoration had been completed.

The Prater Gardens in Vienna had been part of the scenery of the famous Orson Welles movie, 'The Third Man' with its iconic wooden cabined Ferris wheel. In the Gardens there was, probably still is, the Schweitzer House which was famous for its Budweiser beer and food. I understood that the owner of the Schweitzer House had been granted the rights to import draught Budweiser for the whole of Austria from Budovici, in what was then Czechoslovakia and is now, of course, the Czech Republic. Another speciality of the Schweitzer House was their pork knuckle joints served with a sweetish mustard and proper horseradish, not your bottled rubbish. These were served on wooden platters and you could spend half an hour working your way through one of them.

At some point in the past, I believe in the 1930s, a relation of the family who brewed Budweiser had migrated to the USA and started a Budweiser brewery there. I have tried both and there is no comparison. Draft Budweiser from Budovici is like champagne compared to the pale lifeless duplicate from the USA. All a question of taste, I suppose, but for me no competition. I guess my preference is, in part, due to having visited the Budovici brewery and sampled their freshly brewed beer. A party of us from IIASA arrived for an organised tour of the brewery and to be entertained for lunch. Lunch was Hungarian goulash with great chunks of heavy dumplings. However, it all went down just fine accompanied with ample servings of Budweiser beer. The waiters and waitresses serving us continually toured the tables replenishing our small glasses with beer. The glasses probably held no more than two or three mouthfuls of beer but were never empty as they were constantly refilled from large jugs.

During the tour it was explained to us that during the war the Soviet Union had taken the ingredients to brew Budweiser beer back to the Soviet Union, to brew the beer there. However, they missed the crucial ingredient which made the beer so distinctive, the water. There was a well on the site of the brewery which provided all the water that was used in the brewing. Only this water was used in the process in the, what was then the Czechoslovak Republic, so the Soviets never did make the beer as successfully as the Czech's. I guess something similar applies in the UK where, in the Stoke area in the County of Staffordshire—I am not sure if it is still called Staffordshire—but breweries proliferated there where the water was considered the best for beer.

Other successful beers brewed in the Republic were Staropramen and Pilsner Urquel, the latter being brewed in Plzen and is, what is claimed, as the original lager beer. As in Germany, brewing is treated with a great deal of respect in the Czech Republic, and only contains four elements. No chemicals were allowed in their products, I assume this is still the case.

Also, in particular, I remember a visit to Prague for a long weekend with my then partner. Prague in the early 1990s was just starting to emerge from its subservience to Moscow. The city of Prague was virtually undamaged during the Second World War and, as a result of Soviet control, had not been developed in the way that many other cities had been post WW2, being somewhat rundown but scenically beautiful, with magnificent buildings and no tall tenements or new tower blocks, in the centre of the city. The city still retained a feeling of being part of an era of centuries before. As you strolled along, you could hear voices around corners ahead of you and, on turning the corner you half expected to see people dressed as they were two or three centuries earlier. The atmosphere of long ago was palpable.

One morning, my partner and I sat having coffee in a square opposite the enormously ornate town hall clock, again a photograph is included, this was in the famous Prague Old Town Square. As we did so, a quarrel seemed to break out across the street from where we sat. I suddenly had the feeling it was being staged for some reason and became aware that two women close to the scene were acting suspiciously around bystanders. Shortly afterwards, we were strolling up towards the statue of King Wenceslas in Wenceslas Square when we had to crowd together with the other pedestrians onto the pavement to avoid road-works. I was walking on my partner's right side and she had her handbag on her left shoulder. As we squeezed through the narrow gap, I glanced to my left and saw one of the women from the earlier altercation on my partners left looking down and, having unzipped my partner's shoulder bag she was reaching in for the contents. Our passports, cash and credit cards were about to be stolen. Fortunately, because the day had started a bit damp, I had carried an umbrella. It was one of the short ones typically carried by many men. I carried it, not by the curved handle but by the fabric end. Practically screaming at the woman to *"Get your hand out of there"*, I lashed out and smashed the handle onto the back of her hand. I have no feeling of pride for having hit a woman but it was purely reflex and an instinctive reaction to having our money and passports stolen. I doubt that the woman would be stealing anyone's possessions for a while to come. However, I probably frightened my partner as much as the thieving woman and, in part, spoilt what was a wonderful romantic weekend though we both had to smile when the hotel we were staying in produced a bill for the weekend's stay which had written on it, Dr B.W Haywood and one other!

One of the Czech men who had been walking nearby during the attempted pick-pocketing and who spoke perfect English commented that the city was being flooded by particularly Romanian pickpockets, at that time, and congratulated me on my actions, though I felt pretty bad afterwards about hitting the woman. It still is the only time I have ever done such an awful thing.

There were two other non-work related incidents that come to mind, that also provided pleasurable memories. The first was a weekend in Budapest to watch the Hungarian Formula One Grand Prix with a group of about eight or nine friends from the United Nations in Vienna. It was at the time that an English formula one racing driver, a Birmingham chap named Nigel Mansell, was leading the points table and a good performance in Hungary meant he would become that seasons World F1 Champion. He finished second and that was it, Nigel was the Champ. As we drove back in the minibus to Austria from the track and along the motorway, each of the bridges we went under seemed to have Union Jack flags draped over them—not sure where they all came from—and there were cheering groups of people. All the vehicles around us seemed to have Brits heading back towards the border with Austria, with flags hanging out of the windows, and much honking of car horns.

We stopped for a meal close to but just inside the Hungarian border and, because the inside of this very large restaurant was full, we sat at one of the tables outside. One of our party had brought along a life-sized cardboard cut-out of Nigel Mansell in his racing overalls and with a big smile on his face. John Young, for it was he who had brought the cut-out, propped this up facing into the restaurant and a huge cheer went up from inside. I think that, for a moment, the people inside had believed it was the man himself.

As we sat there, parked at the kerb nearby was a very large, very modern touring caravan. As we sat eating and drinking we suddenly became aware that a succession of men were visiting the caravan and it dawned on us it was a mobile brothel! None of our party visited the caravan, though, if the group had been smaller and more inclusive, who knows if anyone would have ventured forth! However, during that weekend in Budapest prior to the race, poor old Roger—I refrain from mentioning his other name out of recognition this might be embarrassing for him—became the butt of our somewhat childish and, perhaps boorish humour. At our hotel bar in Budapest, which was horseshoe-shaped, one of two young ladies sitting opposite sent him a drink. He smiled back at her and the rest of us glanced at each other and smiled. One by one, we left the bar, leaving Roger and the young lady smiling at each other and sharing a drink. Not sure if Roger had twigged at that time that the young lady had ulterior motives, but we assumed that she might have been an occupant of the mobile caravan the following night.

One other thing while working in Vienna was my purchase of what, for me, was something entirely outside my compass, a very expensive car. The first and last such purchase made by myself. In the January of 1991 I, along with many others working at IIASA, had been invited to the unveiling of the brand new model BMW 3 Series car at BMW Wien. We were provided with glasses of champagne and canapés prior to the unveiling. A small Viennese orchestra played music and three motor vehicles were hidden under what looked like silky, grey, parachute style material. The head of BMW from Bayern made a short speech, and with a fanfare from the orchestra and in a cloud of dry ice, the covers slowly rose to reveal three versions of the most beautiful car I had ever seen. It was love at first sight.

Within days my order was in and, in March (at least I think it was March it may have been April) I visited BMW Wien to collect my right-hand drive BMW. No left hand drive BMWs had been delivered in Vienna at that time in my recollection, and because my car had been prepared for the UK market I seemed to be the first person in Vienna to be driving around in the new model, which drew admiring glances wherever I went driving along in my brand new Diamond Black BMW 3 Series.

In may have seemed extravagant to have bought such a car but, as employees of the United Nations, we were offered semi-diplomatic status and did not have to pay the taxes normally associated with such a purchase. Also, my salary at IIASA was quite sufficient to indulge myself for a short period. The car cost the equivalent of £12,000, an enormous sum to me given that, only a few years before, I had been insolvent and trying to pay off all my debts, and even with the concession of the car being tax free. The exact same car with the same specifications in the UK at that time, and with taxes, would have cost between £17,000 and £18,000.

When I returned to the UK, I kept the car for the required twelve months before selling it for exactly the £12,000 I had bought it for due to a short period of unemployment. I had enjoyed what for me was the ultimate driving experience for two years and was sad to see it go but, if I ever manage to win the lottery, look out you folks at BMW I will be back. What do I drive now, here in Cyprus? A fourteen year old, somewhat battered, little white Mitsubishi Mirage. However, it gets me around and it's true to say it has never me given a spot of bother in the almost ten years that I have owned it.

Before completing this section, I should perhaps mention another project, since this was quite similar to the one in Vienna mentioned above, but carried out a little later and not while at UNIDO. This was conducted for the Sectoral Activities Programme of the International Labour Office in Geneva. As a result of my earlier doctoral thesis on the printing industry some fifteen years earlier, I was asked to prepare an international comparison report for the 'Third Tripartite Technical Meeting for the Printing and Allied Trades' examining 'Employment and income in the light of structural and technical changes'. This compared changes in the UK, Japan, Denmark, Yugoslavia, Brazil and the United States. Again, this project was helped by contacts I had made earlier that enabled me to recruit local experts in these disparate countries and again, the project was completed on time, and to the satisfaction of the funding body.

Back to the UK and Brighton University

On returning to the UK, I resumed work with Brighton University for a short period. The contracts I had worked on previously had now been finished and a number of short term contracts were now to be completed. However, my time at Brighton University was coming to an end. Out of funds and employment for several months, this was when the BMW left my ownership. While I liked the concept of being a contract researcher it did have its limitations, such as some contracts only being for a few short months and the longest of my career being three years, However, the main problem being one where most funding bodies or Research Council's having switched off funds, you found yourself unemployed, hence the sale of the BMW.

Eventually, and not too long later, I was able to secure a Senior Fellow's post at Manchester Business School (MBS), working with Professor Peter Barrar in the Operations and Information Development branch of the School.

At that time, not sure what the rankings are now, but MBS was one of the most prestigious business schools and was ranked in the top ten in the world. Most of this work at MBS was conducted for the European Regional Development Fund, focusing on company supply chains, specifically 'Small to Medium Size Company Supply Chains in the North West of England'.

Interviews were carried out and a number of teaching sessions were organised and run, in which companies involved in the research were invited to attend at the School in order to help them understand how they might improve the efficiencies in their individual enterprises. These teaching sessions were enormously successful and resulted in complimentary comments by participants who sent emails or letters to me. An example of several of these, just brief extracts, are reproduced below though full names have been omitted since I have not sought their approval for the use of the quotes, which I am sure would have been forthcoming had I asked. The original communications are available.

'Good Morning Bill, As you got me on to the Internet in the first place and took the trouble to invite me to the Business School, I thought it wholly appropriate that you should receive our first ever e-mail transmission. I have put all new valves in our machine so here goes'. Regards Peter T.

'Dear Bill, I am just writing to say a big thank you for all your help over the past few months. Your courses have been extremely helpful to myself and my father David O. I would also like to thank Robin for his great help especially in getting our web site, not only up and running, but of a very high standard. Good luck for future courses to you and your dedicated team' Julie O.

'Dear Bill, I am writing to thank you for your efforts with introducing information technology to our company. We are currently installing new accounts programmes and have commenced work on design of our first Web-site. We are hoping to attract some overseas customers for our products via the web and we will let you know of our success' Brian H.

These are some of the comments that, fortunately, justify my original goal of obtaining and being able to pass on to others a degree of knowledge that would prove helpful in their own work lives. This whole personal goal started as an attempt to help fellow workers and, indirectly, I believe that the feedback proves it to have been achieved. If these companies are successful, then surely the personnel within them obtain greater job security and enhanced incomes.

I remained with MBS for about five years until, eventually, funding again ran out and another short period of unemployment ensued. Research funding was becoming increasingly tight and only fairly senior staff with a record of successful research and publications were able to elicit funds from the variety of bodies still with money available. Since I was not a professor, and had never seen that as a goal, and had not made many funding applications, I really did not qualify. I much preferred working on the research itself. Let someone else do the more boring job of obtaining the money for the research.

One such person who did qualify as a successful fund raiser through his earlier eminent research was Professor Mick Dunford at the University of Sussex, and this was where I obtained my last full employment before retirement. I was with Mick for a little over two years before reaching the venerable age of 65 and glorious retirement. On being interviewed for the post of Senior Research Fellow, the Head of the School, was apparently unimpressed with my interview and did not wish for me to be appointed. It has to be said that, while I interview others quite successfully, I do not interview well myself, partly I suppose because I am not the most confident person in the world despite the successes I have had in my academic life. I do not interview well, that's the be all, and the end all, of my persona. This is probably down to my inherent insecurity, and the working class background I guess, though I am proud still to label myself as such. Fortunately, Mick was very familiar with my earlier work and carried through my appointment. It was a case, again, of turning the circle. The University of Sussex was where I had obtained my degrees and it was where, almost thirty years later, I was to return to finish my employed period of life. By the time the research was completed, the Head had to admit she was wrong in her objection to my employment, and the research results were, in the words of the assessing body in its End of Award Report, was 'Outstanding'.

The project was entitled 'Regional Economic Performance, Governance and Cohesion in an Enlarged Europe'. It focused on Italy, Slovakia, Poland and the U.K. and was funded by the Economic and Social Research Council (ESRC) in Swindon. Early in the project and before my arrival, there had been difficulties as a result of changing personnel. The researcher responsible for, in part, managing the project and setting up the interviews—the role I was to take over—departed twelve months into the two and a half year project. Also, the Principle Researcher, Dr Adrian Smith, left Sussex for a post at the University of Kentucky in the USA. As a result, much of the project had stalled for about a year.

On my appointment, I took over the role of Senior Researcher and, as Mick who had taken over as Principle Researcher, noted in his final report to the ESRC: 'In January 2001 Bill Haywood started work on the project. From that point onwards rapid progress was made'. The questionnaire survey was completed, as was the programme of interviews. If I am to blow my own trumpet, I was responsible for both setting up the interviews and completing most of them in the UK. It is the kind of thing at which I had become quite proficient. I also carried out contacts with the other international bodies involved in the research and, together with Mick and another colleague, also visited Northern Italy to conduct interviews there.

During the research, and again at the culmination of the project, we held several dissemination seminars which were attended by members of the project team from both the UK and abroad, and also others for whom it was considered important to keep well informed. I was responsible for arranging these meetings and the production of the final meeting proceedings. I have to confess here that I have always loved being in charge of things during my time as a researcher. Working almost as a project manager on this research was right up my street and followed on from my work with IIASA and UNIDO in Austria, and at the Manchester Business School. At that time,

I liked nothing better than organising things and the feeling of being in control of what I was doing. This did not make me a despot since I had no real control over others, though there were usually research assistants working with me, merely that I could just get on with things without interruption after chatting with Mick about my intentions.

Almost the whole of my last twenty years or so of employment was essentially in a project management role, whether that was formalised or otherwise. In general, I was left to get on with the job on which I was employed and always this seemed to prove successful.

Suddenly, I have this very nasty feeling that much of what is written so far, almost from page one is a kind of blowing my own trumpet diatribe. It was not, or is not, meant to be that. Really I should reiterate that the whole emphasis of what is laid down in this autobiography is meant to offer some modicum of encouragement to others not to just accept a life in a factory, or an office, or a shop. Maybe just outside that factory/office/shop door fate holds something for you that you had never contemplated? There are opportunities out there, I guess you just need to try and to be a little lucky. Though the odds are against anyone from a more, shall we say deprived background, never despair. As noted earlier, it seems to me that a country's economic success depends on the education, skills and health of its population, especially when its young people are healthy and well educated, and that they can find gainful employment and achieve dignity and success in their lives.

For myself, and looking back, I have this feeling that, when I started that correspondence course with Sam Rouse, it was a bit like stepping into soft snow at the top of a mountain and getting slowly carried away. At Ruskin College, the slide seemed to get faster and I was led onwards without too much control. At university it became an avalanche which never seemed likely to end until my retirement.

Life beyond academia

It seems that most of what life, or at least that part of it noted above, had held in store for me from the age of 35 through until retirement age, was focused on education and a progression through work with various national and international educational and/or government bodies, with moments of humour, sport, and dare I admit it, gambling. However, this is definitely not the whole story. There were other very important events in my life, some more important than others but all obviously of relevance to me personally, there have been moments of relationships that will not be discussed here. Not all of my experiences have been laid down here in this little story. As for all of us, there were more personal moments that need to be kept between individuals, or are perhaps just intended to maintain a degree of reflection not shared by others. Show me a person who declares they have no secrets in their life and I will show you someone who is deluded!

As you will have gathered, having got this far in my life story, sport has in many ways sustained me.

Football, horse racing, darts, athletics, and so on. I took part in and enjoyed them all. Some of the more sedentary I still do, since age has tended to take its toll as it does with us all eventually. The idea of running around on a football pitch no longer has the appeal it once had, strong as that was at the time. Now, it's just watching a game that I no longer recognise as the sport when I was a participant. I still watch games, especially my beloved Baggies, but most of the time I do so somewhat ruefully.

All of these more prosaic pastimes were not crucially important but part and parcel of the life that I have managed to lead with some measure of success. There were times when the pressure of meeting deadlines in research schedules needed the outlet of these, perhaps to some, more boring opportunities. There were occasions when working twelve hour days to meet such tight schedules did become onerous, and as I noted earlier, on at least two occasions I had to step aside from academic work to ease that mental pressure. However, I never did manage to have a mental breakdown so maybe I got away with the pressures somewhat lightly.

There were other major moments unrelated to work. I have no intention of relating the more intimate events since I believe that there is far too much of the 'kiss and tell' element in the media, which should be of no interest to anyone but the people concerned. While the above is true for myself, I am not entirely sure if it is true for many others since much of what appears in the more, shall I say, lurid red top dailies appears a love of delving into the more salacious lives of other people, especially those who are too lightly described as 'celebrities', people who trundle on to those abominable in-house shows and reality shows.

However, Muriel, Suzie, Rita, Anne, and Renata, amongst a few others, were all important parts of my life in some form or another during all these years. And, no, I am not like Coronation Streets Ken Barlow's alter-ego, I believe his name is William Roache. It seems odd that someone of such an age as 'Ken' feels a need to explain to all and sundry his 'success' with a multitude of the opposite sex. Where does love seem to have disappeared to in all this? Can you truly love five hundred or a thousand women? Is it merely ego that makes such 'stars' as 'Ken' or Spanish singer 'Julio Inglesias', whose proclaimed 'successes' with the ladies has been broadcast to all and sundry? Did they claim these 'successes' with the ladies themselves, or is this all a figment of some journalists imagination?

There have not been one thousand women in my life, or even five hundred, far, far from it! Frankly, it seems to me that sex for sex's sake belongs to a rather shallow world. For me, making love is to be in love. Sex without love is I feel a chimera and I feel somewhat sorry for all those so-called celebrities who loudly proclaim their 'achievements' in those terms.

Perhaps, once again, the above sounds very priggish and prudish, I can't help it, it is just my own personal perception. To say otherwise would be dishonest and honesty ranks very high in my personal criteria. Each of the women I have known, and not necessarily in the biblical sense, has been important in their own way and I have no wish to embarrass or intrude further into their lives. Needless to say, these ladies were as important to me as the education and employment that surrounded both them and me. I hope that some, if not all of them, can look back with some degree of friendship to the time we knew each other.

I must confess, however, that the more personal relationships in my life have never lasted for much more than about four years. I put this down to various reasons. One is that, as I noted earlier, I guess I am a rather selfish person. I doubt that I could have achieved the education I have, and the employment and travel that followed, if I had had a wife and children accompanied by all of the financial constraints of mortgages, hire purchase, and other financial commitments. While working at GKN, I was surrounded by fellow workers with at least my level of ability during the summer months when I returned to GKN in 1975. I tried to encourage some of them to follow my example and try for further education. To a man, they could not because of their family commitments of said children's education, along with the mortgages, hire purchase debts, and so on. As a bachelor with no family or financial liabilities, I was able to do as I wished so that, even if this meant I went into debt that was my problem to solve. I must admit, though, that I was assisted importantly by the support of the lads on the shop floor at GKN during 1974/75 as I described above, and as importantly by the financial and moral support of my sister Edna.

Probably another reason for my rather short-term relationships is that I am not a terribly ambitious person. I had no desire for the prestige of a professor's Chair. I have always felt I was privileged to have escaped working in factories for the whole of my working life and experiencing the things that I eventually did. I earned a decent living doing something I loved doing. Perhaps there are not that many people who can say that with their hand on their heart. It may well be that I lacked ambition as some may see it, and that has certainly been expressed to me by some of the women in my life, but that's just me. I really did not, and do not, wish to change into something that I am not. Why strive for, and perhaps become disillusioned by, failing to achieve more than you need in life? Modern money-grabbers might find that attitude absolutely impossible to believe. Maybe that is why I find grasping for more and more money and possessions, so incomprehensible. I have a small home that is my own here in Cyprus. My pension is sufficient to maintain my very moderate life style. I do not need to have half a dozen cars. You can only drive one at a time and, while I miss my BMW3, the Mitsubishi Mirage gets me around quite satisfactorily—old as it may be!

I guess, this is another of the other reasons why I have never married: I am not sure whether it's just me but some of the women involved in my life, after a short period of delight, at least it was for me, seem to have wanted to change me into something that I am not. Do many men find this to be the case? Maybe this is a research project that someone should undertake, or perhaps they already have and I am unaware of it. How about you women out there? Are the men in your life attempting to change you into something you are not? Is this an activity that is prevalent between the sexes? I seem to recall reading somewhere in the dim and distant past that, when a man marries a woman, he hopes she will stay the same forever but, when a woman marries a man, her agenda is to change him! That may sound cynical coming from a man but from my experience it has some validity.

The proposal that women come from Venus and men from Mars is a complex one but its clear there are significant psychological differences, quite apart from the biological ones. But, is this a true difference between the sexes or merely in the heads of the individuals, irrespective of, and unrelated to, their individual sex. While I was at Sussex University as a student, there was a married couple where the man was undertaking a degree and his wife worked at the university as a porter in order to support him and his miserly grant. When he graduated, his wife wanted to take a degree herself and believed quite rightly that he should help support her. He left her. Maybe he could not face the idea that she was as intelligent and as desirous of wanting to be educated as he was himself. Not quite sure how exactly that relates to the paragraphs above, but I think there is something in it somehow if I think hard enough!

A professor's Chair or other awards, or more money, was never my driving ambition. Perhaps it sounds a little pretentious to say that the accumulation and diffusion of knowledge was uppermost in my mind, but I guess that is closest to the truth. What is it that drives any individual forward? If that concept could be bottled, anyone who achieved it would make a fortune! Its sad that we spend so much time in our lives gathering knowledge as individuals, then we die and that knowledge for the most part dies with us. The knowledge written on what was the original 'tabula rasa' of that individual is erased forever, unless they were fortunate enough to be able to leave to posterity their thoughts in the printed word or in some other medium.

Not many people actually get to leave an imprint on history. People such as presidents and kings, great artists and major sports personalities, peacemakers, society changers and philosophers may succeed, but many others, perhaps most others, are remembered only by the people who knew them at the personal level. Admittedly, in my case, there are a few pieces of written material that float around with my name on them, but they are all of a technical and academic, and specific nature and unlikely to thrill anyone dramatically. When all of those people who know me or knew me themselves die, my life will be as nothing just like most of those people in the world who are not recognised for anything auspicious!

Does that sound too gloomy and depressing? Not at all. For me, it is a fact of life and we would all be much happier if we could accept that that is what life is all about. I find it easy to accept since, for the most part, I consider myself without religious feelings and accept I am a humanist by nature. I believe in people and, though they can let you down, to lose that optimism would be a sad thing. For me, we are born, we live for a specific period of time and we die. I suppose it would be nice to be a Buddhist and believe that, at the end of one's current life, there is merely a pause before transition and re-birth. I do not have that concept within me. Do we have a soul that lingers after death and is transferred into another body? I doubt it very much. This concept may give solace to some who cannot believe that there is nothing beyond their current existence but for me, it is a concept I cannot embrace.

Again, perhaps some people may consider that my personal views are those of a cynic. Not so. I have enjoyed, and continue to enjoy, the life so far led. Perhaps if I had suffered some devastating loss in my life or had been unfortunate enough to have suffered some physical or mental illness, I would have thought otherwise but I guess, yet again, that I have been lucky. In the past, being a Senior Research Fellow was the extent of my ambition. I was travelling extensively through the UK, and the rest of the world, carrying out work I loved doing, and meeting fascinating people. I received a reasonable salary to sustain me without this being anything excessive. A life lived which is full of regrets for what might have been is a life wasted in my view. I would have loved to have been a professional footballer but fate decreed otherwise. I did not have to work in a factory all my life and did a job I enjoyed. What is to regret? I saw places such as Rio de Janeiro, Sao Paulo, Prague, Bratislava, Budapest, New York, Rome, Milan, Paris, Warsaw, Copenhagen, Stockholm, Helsinki, Vienna and many other beautiful cities.

If that first step on the slippery slope of further and higher education had not taken place, none of this would have happened and maybe I would have ended up a bit of a cynic after another thirty years of soldering on in factories? Or, even worse, to have spent half a lifetime without work and being inadequately sustained, and possibly being vilified for being dependant on the State as so many people are in this era in the UK. However, unfortunately, some of the women in the more personal relationships I was involved in seemed more intent on my climbing upwards, earning more money and attaining more prestige. I have to confess that the female of the species, or at least some of the ones briefly noted above, seemed more ambitious for their man than the man was himself! Was it ever thus?

Is there a woman in my life now? No. Do I regret this? Yes and no. I am rapidly approaching my seventy sixth birthday and have long been retired, but I still miss cuddling up to some attractive, intelligent, sexy woman in bed so, yes, I do miss this. However, I suspect my appeal to the opposite sex is something that expired many years ago. I do not kid myself that I am the answer to anyone's dream or prayer, if I ever was. However, to see a woman's gentle smile when I kiss her neck, while she is lying still asleep in my arms, or to feel her heart beating beneath the palm of my hand what a glorious sensation. To walk down the street with my arm around her waist is, or should I say was, worth far more than prestige or money. You see I am, after all, a kind of old-fashioned bloke, as I am sure has quite clearly come across in many of my views expressed above. I suspect that under the rather selfish exterior a little bit of a romantic if you can tap into it. There, you have it. To me, it is the little things like the above that do matter, and that I do miss in personal relationships.

For what it is worth to you members of the younger generations, the fire never entirely dies, though it may become more contained, at least for some of us. You should be very, very glad that it does. I find it very amusing that younger people seem to find the idea of the, what I will call the 'more elderly', still seem to enjoy a good old cuddle now and then—and whisper it softly, maybe a little more than a good old cuddle!

My failure to be in a current relationship comes back to that innate selfishness that I have continually stressed. If I want to do something or go somewhere I still want the freedom to do so as I wish and without having to consider anyone or anything else. I admit it, I am utterly self contained and selfish! I am tempted to say that I do not value relationships above the freedom to act as I wish, so there you have my dilemma. Despite my being reasonably content with my life, I am somewhat constrained by my failing to win the lottery since retiring and that's a shame because I guess that some part of me would still rather like to be a millionaire and travel around the world, indulging myself by watching cricket in the West Indies, or going over to Australia to watch the Melbourne Cup. Maybe if I were a millionaire it would even make me more attractive to the female of the species! Just kidding and showing that more cynical side that I have been trying to conceal. Paradoxically, I want both the sort of relationship I have described above and yet to retain the freedom to please myself. Maybe I have a sort of split personality and I am not sure there are women out there who would or could tolerate such a self-centred person as myself. Maybe it's why women disappear from my life after about four years. Maybe it is not me that ends it all, but I certainly contribute to the changes in circumstances.

So, how do I occupy myself in my retirement? Like all 'lotus eaters' who have retired to sunnier climes I lounge in the sun and drink more than I should, but what the hell, who else cares if I am a little overweight and feel the need to indulge myself? Why am I here living in Cyprus, where the sunnier climes exist and the cold beer and good book are to hand? I still read prolifically, and sitting in the sun with a cold beer near-by and a good book or newspaper in my hand (see the final photograph in the book), is almost enough but not quite.

Back in the UK, one Sunday afternoon and shortly after retiring and having moved back to the West Midlands, from my little flat in Brighton, I sat in my little terraced house and stared down the back garden through the patio windows. It was in December 2003 and the sky was grey and darkening, and a steady drizzle of rain soaked the grass outside. I thought to myself 'Why on earth am I sitting here in this grey depressing gloom, when there is a wide world out there', much of which I had already seen. The seed was sown and a few weeks later, I went on holiday to Spain with the thought that I might want to move there. The resort was Benalmadena—not sure of the spelling—but it was awful. There were tower blocks of flats, and virtually every shop and restaurant staffed by ex-Pat's, many of whom were quite surly. Now I like my fellow Brit's in small portions, but this was like the worst type of English seaside resort, only with sunshine.

A couple of months later it was time for a two week holiday here in Cyprus, where I had spent almost two years of my RAF service in my late teens and early twenties, as I recounted above. Within days it felt like home. The weather was wonderful and the sun shines 330 or so days of the year. The third apartment I viewed I loved, with its view over the banana plantation and thence over the sea. I sold my little house in Wednesbury, West Midlands—I still like to think of the area as Staffordshire as it was before its growth into a conurbation—and have been over here in Cyprus ever since. A complete return to the UK is unlikely until the day of my demise. Maybe they will scatter my ashes over the Albion football pitch? Here I can look out of the window and see the Mediterranean, the blue skies and the sunshine, and Cyprus really has become my home. Normally, I return to the UK for about one month each year, during August when the temperatures over here usually exceed 100 degrees and the humidity is rather hard to take. This allows me the opportunity to visit relatives, with whom I usually stay, since I no longer have property in the UK.

I am still a complete sports freak. Virtually any sport will have me glued to the TV screen, urging on any Englishman or Englishwoman engaged in any sport. And, yes, I do support my other fellow Brits, but not quite as enthusiastically as I do the English variety. Whisper it quietly, but I can't stand the ultra-competitive sportsmen who believe that winning is the be all and end all. I have to confess, I cannot abide many Australian cricketers for this very reason.

Is my aversion to Australian cricketers reasonable? Can I sustain this with argument? Yes, I believe I can under my own terms of reference. The Aussies conceived of the idea of 'sledging'. No, not as in winter sports, sledging in this context comprises not of concentrating on the cricket itself, but on mentally upsetting the opposition players. Insulting relatives or the individual player's, seem to be the options. Of course, the Australians are no longer the only exponents of this abuse, now most teams indulge, and not just cricketers, but the Aussies were the innovators and are still the experts, something of which they seem inordinately proud.

It should be noted that the Manager of the Australian team, even before the English team left for Australia this year (2013), was encouraging spectators back in Australia to abuse one of the English players who refused to walk off the pitch when he was clearly out, but not given out by the Umpires, during an earlier series in the UK. Strange that following that incident several retired and rather more elderly Australian ex-test match players have observed they would have done exactly the same as the English player in similar circumstances. For them it was up to the Umpires to make the decision and to stand by that decision. I do not justify the action of the English cricketer, but it seems that what has become increasingly normal in many sports is to play mind games with the opposition. In that late 2013, early 2014 Ashes test series, I believe it was in Melbourne actually, one of the English cricketers who clearly suffered under some mental stress was continually hounded by one particular Australian. This was a man who deemed it appropriate to attempt to physically assault another England cricketer in an earlier off-field incident back in the UK. Similarly, I believe it was in the same test match, the Aussie captain, Clarke, issued threats to have another English player's arm broken by his fast bowlers, and this verbal attack was not against a first rank batsman but to a tail-end batsman who was far less likely to be able to fend for himself while at the crease. This, from the captain of the team, who should have been leading by example in fair play and sportsmanship. Wasn't cricket supposed to embody the very epitome of sportsmanship? A gentleman's game? No longer, I fear.

It can be argued that both of the Australians were provoked. Not being religious myself, I believe that I recall Jesus saying something about turning the other cheek? I cannot believe that such humility exists in many Australian cricketers concept's, it is just not macho enough. Perhaps the fact that they had lost the previous three test series was a contributing factor in their increasingly aggressive actions. Personally, I think if winning is that important to the Australians, I suggest we just pass that little Ashes trophy over to them to keep. Perhaps they can find another international team to play who adopt the same approach to 'Sport'. It seems to me, and of course this is a personal opinion, that calling many Australian cricketers sportsmen is a contradiction in terms. It's funny but I seem to recall that the man who created the concept of the modern Olympics believed that it was not the winning that counted but the taking part. I may not have his name spelt correctly but I believe his name was something like Baron Pierre de Coubertin, a man after my own heart. Maybe I am a loser after all?

Yes, I admit it, I am at base an Englishman of the old school and I believe in sportsmanship and fair play. I think that is something to be proud of and not ashamed of. We may, in our colonial past, not have been the perfect people in seeking to control others through an empire and/or running other people's lives but, on occasion, we have left certain good things behind when we have left these countries and these have included some measure of good works. It appears that, unlike many other 'Empires' of the past, we did at least leave most of these colonies willingly rather than under duress. Why, otherwise, are countries such as Canada and New Zealand, even India which is a country which we probably most exploited, still part of the Commonwealth of Nations? Nowadays, the colonial powers we see are largely of the financial type, the USA, China, Russia, and perhaps increasingly Germany. Many of these countries now seek to overtly obtain control of other states through financial clout, rather than through the bullet and the bomb, though it has to be said that some of them do not exclude the latter, either in tangible forms or by ulterior intervention and proxy.

One example of this at the time of writing is the activity of the Russian Federation. It has already pretty well annexed Georgia, and is now performing the same action in the Ukraine in the take-over of the Crimea. Do people recall the Sudetenland example of such actions? After the First World War this border area between Germany and Czechoslovakia was ceded to Czechoslovakia. The fact that most of the people from the area were German speaking was used by Germany to justify its annexation in 1938. What followed is history, and what do they say about history? If you do not learn from it, you are likely to repeat it!

However, enough of my personal social reflections and back to my main sporting weakness, which is my continuing passion for horse racing. Right from an early age I have been a punter and the urge has never left me. How's that, Dad? This little tale is littered with stories of my taking on the bookmakers. Am I a successful punter, of course I am not entirely a winner, few punters are. If punters tell you they regularly make money from gambling just take that with a pinch of salt, the majority certainly do not. I do have my days, however, and I will relate one occasion where there were a few exceptional days all rolled together.

While a 49-year-old student at Sussex University, still working for my doctorate and with a £2,000 overdraft at the bank, a friend, who ran his own business in Brighton and was like me a horse racing addict, called to say he was going over to the Arc de Triomphe race meeting at Longchamp in Paris, and taking his girlfriend. There was room for one more in his

E-type Jag if I wanted to come with them. This was in October 1986, as I recall. Incredibly that's almost 28 years ago; doesn't time fly when you get to the latter stages of your life. Anyhow I told him no, and explained I could not afford it and was overdrawn at the bank, but, in fact, that I longed to go and that if anything changed, I would give him a call.

Two days before his Saturday afternoon departure for France, there was a race meeting at Newmarket on the Thursday. Give it a go, I thought, so I visited a cash-point machine and increased my £2,000 overdraft by another £70. I must have been mad, or maybe I was inspired, or perhaps Lady Luck was merely looking over my shoulder, and felt I needed a little boost in my life. Visiting a Ladbrokes betting shop, I placed a £10 win patent bet: that is three £10 win singles, three £10 win doubles and a £10 win treble. I have a photocopy of the betting slip by my side on the desk right now, and a photograph of this is included in the book. It reads:

Gold Fee won 6/4
Verd Antique won 11/2
Clarentia won 12/1

I had won £3,664, and phoned my colleague to confirm that circumstances had changed, and that I would be going to the Arc with them. The following day, I went to the bookmakers and collected my winnings. I visited my bank and deposited £3,000 wiping out my overdraft and leaving a healthy balance in its place.

I left just over £260 at home and, on the Saturday afternoon, he picked me up and we drove to Newhaven for the ferry to France. On the way over on the ferry we had a meal and drinks and tossed a coin to see who paid. I lost: £40 bill to pay. One tenth of my gambling money was gone. Stopping halfway to Paris we stayed that Saturday night in a hotel. I believe it was in some cathedral city but the name escapes me, was it Rheims? It might have been. Fortunately he paid for the rooms so I was OK there, still with a few pounds in my pocket.

Arriving in Paris we parked the car and, for 10 Francs each, the equivalent at that time of £1.10p or £1.20p, we entered the racecourse with access to all parts of the course except for the seventh tier of the grandstand that was reserved to owners and trainers, and their guests. As an aside, entry at Brighton racecourse, which was about half a mile away from where I lived at that time, cost £12 per person, and that was not the most expensive enclosure!

My colleague, who was about six foot four inches tall and built like the proverbial out-house, hustled to the front of the queue in the ground floor restaurant of the seven-tier grandstand. He tapped the Maitre D' on his shoulder and the man turned round looked up into his face and quickly had one of the waiters take us to a table overlooking the track. This meant that we had the table for the entire day. I understand that even if we had left halfway through racing they would not have used that table again. Apparently, that was the normal procedure. The three-course meal that took several hours to consume in the relaxed atmosphere that prevailed, cost £45 per head. Hard to believe that, in addition to the half bottle of wine which came with each meal, we consumed seven bottles of champagne over the following seven hours, and his girlfriend did not like champagne so it was consumed by my friend and me! Over the course of the meeting my colleague, who had taken £1,000 with him had lost on every race and was what we termed pot-less. Not a penny to his name. Lady Luck was not on his side that day. The meal and drinks bill came to the equivalent of £450, more than I had even started out the day with. Would we end up washing dishes for the next week, or month, I thought? It all depended on how I came out at the end of the race meeting and my wagers.

In the first race I had won 450 Francs on a 20/1 placed horse. The horse finished second and I also noted another improving horse in the race that I backed ante-post in the following year's 1,000 Guineas classic at Newmarket. The filly, called Miesque, won that 1987 1,000 Guineas race and went on to be a champion racehorse. In the third race I had a fairly hefty bet on an English horse by the name of Double Schwartz. This won the Prix de l'Abbaye sprint at short odds, I think it was about 2/1. On the next race I had another winner, though the name escapes me on that one, but I was well up by the time of the big race and placed 2000 francs, that was the equivalent of around £200 at that time, on the English champion Dancing Brave in his pink and green colours. Dancing Brave was trained by Guy Harwood and ridden by Pat Eddery. Three horses opened up as joint favourites in the Prix de l'Arc de Triomphe: the French champion, called Bering, the German champion, Acatanengo, and the English champion, Dancing Brave. Dancing Brave won, the third horse home behind Dancing Brave and Bering was Triptych which also went on to be a champion horse, that horse was French trained as well. However, prior to the race starting there was heavy support for Dancing Brave by the large number of Brits on the course, which meant he started at slightly odds on.

Dancing Brave won the race quite easily. It was estimated that there were over 50,000 people present on the track and up to a third of these were thought to be Brits so, as the horse strode through on the outside and into the lead in the last furlong a huge roar went up. Another approximate 2,200 francs profit added to my pot. Dancing Brave was a wonderful horse and should have won the English Derby before going for the Arc de Triomphe. Poor old Greville Starkey, who rode the horse that day in the Derby, was castigated for the poor timing of his late run to the post and was beaten into second place and, because of this lost the chance of the winning ride in the Arc. In the next race the Prix de l'Opera, I backed another winner and won another 2000 francs. I even managed to find the winner of the last race the Prix de la Concorde, and added another 1,500 francs.

Time to settle up the bill in the restaurant, and as I mentioned earlier, my friend was pot-less. I counted out the equivalent of £450 plus a hefty tip and, at 7pm, we exited the track with no thought of having to do the washing up. Despite the seven bottles of champagne we both felt quite sober since we had been relaxing and eating throughout the afternoon and he drove the three of us back to Dieppe quite safely. We continued to drink on the ferry, paid for by yours truly since I was the only one with money in my pocket, though how much I had no clue. Was I resentful at having to foot the bill at the restaurant? Of course not, if the boot had been on the other foot, he would have paid up just as happily. In fact he paid the bill quite happily on other occasions when we went racing back in the UK. The weekend had been a huge success for the three of us.

By the time I was dropped off at home in Brighton it was in the early hours of Monday morning, I fell into bed feeling quite drunk after the numerous drinks on the ferry. The following morning I awoke and, after a quick cup of tea, emptied my pockets to count up what remained of my money. I had taken £400 with me to France and now had well over £450 in cash laid out before me. I had had a fabulous weekend that I would remember for the rest of my life. After all, it is now almost 28 years later and I still feel good writing about it and, yes, I had also returned with more money than when I left which of course helped. It does not get much better than this where horse racing is concerned, or when any memorable weekend is concerned and, yes, I confess there have been a few memorable weekends in Vienna, Budapest and the capital of the Czech republic, Prague, a beautiful city which holds very fond and romantic memories.

If you're not tired of my love of horse racing there is another tale to tell and I think this contains a little bit of a moral element, which states that cheaters are not always the winners. What is that old saying? Cheats never prosper. Well, in this case he certainly did not. My favourite race course in the UK has to be Goodwood in Sussex. The festival meeting, situated in beautiful countryside with views over the course to die for, is usually held at the end of July and/or the beginning of August when the weather usually conspires to be fantastic, leading to the expression Glorious Goodwood.

One day, I went to the racecourse with £60 in my pocket and managed to lose £40 on the first two races. The third race on the card was a sprint handicap with about twenty runners. 'In for a penny in for a pound' I thought, 'probably destined for an early exit from the track'. My last twenty pounds went as a £10 each-way bet on a horse which I seem to recall was ridden by Lester Piggott. The horse finished fourth but, because it was a handicap race with a big field, the bookmakers were paying out on the fourth horse as well. I waited to be paid out and I presented my ticket to the bookmaker only to be told there was nothing back, my horse had lost. Lost? It was fourth and therefore a winning bet. He had started to rip up the ticket but I snatched it back and strode away with it. He probably thought that was it. Wrong. I hate cheats as you may already have gathered. Going up to the rear of the stands I saw a racecourse official and explained what had happened. He directed me to an office and knocking on the door, I found it opened by a rather large gentleman. In fact, he filled the doorway. I presented the ticket to him and explained again what had happened. *"Oh him"*, he said, and reached for his hat.

You now have to try to visualise what followed. He had to stoop to come through the door. He wore a camel hair overcoat despite a temperature in the low 90s, and, with his bowler hat on looked about seven foot tall. He gave the distinct impression of being an ex-Guards officer about to set off on a new campaign, which he seemed to be relishing. I can only describe it as perhaps feeling like being one of the Israelites as they followed Moses through the alleged, parted, Red Sea. The huge packed crowd in front of the grandstands seemed to roll back in front of him as he headed for the rails, with me scurrying behind as he went straight for the bookmaker. Snatching the book from the bookmaker's clerk he looked at my ticket number and ran his finger down the entries. *"What's this"*, he growled, and glared at the bookmaker, who had gone through several shades of white and now looked distinctly greenish. The bookmaker, of course,

tried to blame his clerk for the error. He gave me my
£40 because my horse had been 12/1 and at a quarter
of the odds this meant I had doubled my money.
*"One more instance of sharp practice from you and your
licence will be gone"*, my benefactor declared to the
bookmaker. It should be said that a bookmaker's pitch,
as they are called, can be worth several thousand's
pounds. I believe that some are sold for as much
as £10,000 at the more illustrious tracks such as
Goodwood, Epsom and Ascot.

However, this was not the end of the story. As I noted
above, I hate cheats in any form or guise whether it
be at football or horse racing or in any other capacity.
In the next race, I had picked out a short-priced horse
that I really fancied and staked my £40. The cheating
bookie had the best odds available so he took my
money, without comment. The horse won at 2/1 and
I now had £120 to my name, double that with which
I had entered the racetrack. Again, he did not say a
word as I picked up my money. By now, I was really
up to do this man some mischief. The next race was a
two mile handicap in which, if my memory serves me
well, I fancied a 10/1 shot called Golden Fire ridden
by a jockey by the name of Fox. I had £10 each way,
same Bookie, and it won. More bitten lip, by this poor
unfortunate fellow. The final race of the day was a
sprint race and my fancy was ridden by Scobie Breasley

or Lester Piggott, cannot remember which. I had £100 at even money with my mate the bookie, and it won. I think he had been afraid to refuse my bets in case I went and fetched my mate the seven foot guardsman. I walked away from the track with over £400 in my pocket and I would not mind betting that bookmaker wished he had paid me out the legitimate £40 that I had originally won, and that I had gone away and never crossed his path again.

One other result of my earlier confrontation with this bookmaker was that a number of interested bystanders had been intrigued by me and the camel hair-coated giant's confrontation with the bookmaker. I noticed that, when I went back to place wagers with him, a number of those interested bystanders who I recognised, followed me up to place bets. Not sure if they backed the same horse as myself but, if they did he was hit even worse. Perhaps a salutary lesson in the case of the biter bit.

Rounding up the lessons learnt

Having spent a few months and arrived towards the end of this little autobiography, I was forced to start to rethink why I had bothered to consider writing my autobiography in the first place. After all, I said I would never work again once I was retired. However, as I noted on virtually the first page, I did feel that maybe there just might be one or two people out there who, given the opportunity to read this, might take heart and have a go themselves at reaching for the alleged unreachable. I already know of two people I have spoken to in previous years about what life had held in store for me personally, who have themselves, reached out and done the same for themselves. Even if those two are the only ones to do so, perhaps that was reason enough for me to try to put my experiences down on paper in the hope perhaps others would follow my lead. Who knows, perhaps having read this little effort, someone else will try to follow on and change their lives. It is a small hope of mine.

However, what was it that started me on this somewhat bizarre route from being totally unqualified with a foreshortened education as a child through early, not very successful schooling, to industry, the RAF and academia? Yes, I guess I do have some ability; yes, I do feel the need to do whatever I can to be the best I can be, without compromising my own integrity but it does need a spark to set a light to that flame. I guess, in part, it was becoming a shop steward at GKN, in part it was restarting an education that had never really taken off as a youngster partly because of the system and that era in the 1940s and 1950s. In part, it was the huge amount of encouragement provided by my early correspondence course tutor, Sam Rouse, and the stimulation and the listening to and learning from people like the inspirational Chris Freeman and others.

Another element has only now occurred to me as being relevant, while writing this particular part of the story. In my early thirties I picked up a book from some second-hand book stall. It was called 'A Cage of Shadows' and was written by a Black Country poet, and author and journalist, by the name of Archie Hill. I still read this book at least once a year because I find it inspirational. I heartily recommend it, though maybe as a Black Country lad myself, it speaks to me in ways that may not affect others from other parts of the United Kingdom so strongly since, in part, it is written in the Black Country vernacular and talks about places I remember and that still feel familiar. The book tells Archie's life story from being a youngster in the Black Country, my part of the country and of which I am proud, during the depression. It describes how ordinary working class people struggled to live, at a time when there was little or no employment, and tells of the games that had to be played in order to secure food or coal for heating their houses, during a time of employer lock-outs.

In the book, there is one hilarious story about stealing a pig from a local farm and the almost diabolically funny attempts to kill it: chasing it down the street when it managed to escape, with the furore of the beast's charge down the street after it had escaped, and ending with it eventually being killed by a passing lorry, and of the subsequent dispersing of joints of meat through the local community. The book contains moments of humour like this that might seem as black as the area of the country that it comes from. It reveals both despair and hope for the future. It tells the story of ordinary folk and their struggles.

Archie tells of his growing up, of his friends and the little things that meant so much to him as a child, like a little glass ornament made for him when he was a youngster by some kind old gent working in a shed in his back garden. He recounts of how he became first a soldier and then a policeman and, during all of his adult life, of his deep-seated alcoholism. He ended up at one stage, living under the bridges of London and drinking any form of alcohol he could lay his hands on, including methylated spirits, something he quite openly admitted. Despite all of this deprived past and drunken despair, Archie broke with his history and with alcohol because of the kindness of one person who looked beyond the alcoholic who stood before him, and held out a helping hand. With a little luck, in addition, he eventually obtained a job as a reporter with a local newspaper. He moved onwards and upwards, eventually working for what was then called the *Manchester Guardian*, and is, of course, the present day *Guardian*. He wrote several books, another which I also have is called 'A Corridor of Mirrors'. Archie eventually married and had a disabled son upon whom he doted, and Archie thrived despite his past.

Maybe Archie Hill was also part of the stimulus for my wanting not to become a 'Slave to a machine' as my old GKN colleague Arthur so eloquently expressed it, without my being aware of it at the time. Maybe we need more than one stimulus. Perhaps I am becoming too analytical at this point. Sometimes, perhaps it's a question of who knows what drives us to certain actions!

Two men had most to do with my development from my mid 30s until my mid 40s, these were, Sam Rouse and Chris Freeman. I remain eternally grateful to both of them. Maybe Archie Hill's words were also a driving force. Of equal importance in the transformation of my life was the role of my sister Edna. She was the one who offered encouragement and financial support over the years.

For all of this, I will remain eternally grateful. I dedicate this little tome to the four of them: Edna, Sam, Chris and Archie; with the reminder that the fact that I managed, even at such a late stage of my life, to go to Ruskin College where I learnt so much, and then went on to university; to travel extensively worldwide and visit so many interesting places; to learn quite a lot as a result of these developments and interactions has only made me realise that, only now have I been made aware of just how little I really do know